Media Servers for Lighting Programmers

Media Servers for Lighting Programmers

Programmers

A Comprehensive Guide to Working with Digital Lighting

Vickie Claiborne

Focal Press
Taylor & Francis Group

NEW YORK AND LONDON

First published 2014
by Focal Press
70 Blanchard Road, Suite 402, Burlington, MA 01803

and by Focal Press
2 Park Square, Milton Park, Abingdon, Oxon OX14 4RN

Focal Press is an imprint of the Taylor & Francis Group, an informa business

© 2014 Taylor & Francis

Notices
Knowledge and best practice in this field are constantly changing. As new research
and experience broaden our understanding, changes in research methods, professional practices, or medical treatment may become necessary.

Practitioners and researchers must always rely on their own experience and knowledge in evaluating and using any information, methods, compounds, or experiments
described herein. In using such information or methods they should be mindful
of their own safety and the safety of others, including parties for whom they have a
professional responsibility.

Product or corporate names may be trademarks or registered trademarks, and are
used only for identification and explanation without intent to infringe.

Library of Congress Cataloging in Publication Data
Claiborne, Vickie.
Media servers for lighting programmers : a comprehensive guide to working with
digital lighting by Vickie Claiborne.
pages cm
1. Cinematography—Lighting—Automatic control. 2. Stage lighting—Automatic
control. 3. Electric lighting—Automatic control. 4. Digital control systems. I. Title.
TR891.C53 2014
777′.52—dc23   2013031890

ISBN: 978-0-415-72189-9 (pbk)
ISBN: 978-1-315-85894-4 (ebk)

Typeset in ITC Giovanni Std
By MPS Limited, Chennai, India

Bound to Create

You are a creator.

Whatever your form of expression — photography, filmmaking, animation, games, audio, media communication, web design, or theatre — you simply want to create without limitation. Bound by nothing except your own creativity and determination.

Focal Press can help.

For over 75 years Focal has published books that support your creative goals. Our founder, Andor Kraszna-Krausz, established Focal in 1938 so you could have access to leading-edge expert knowledge, techniques, and tools that allow you to create without constraint. We strive to create exceptional, engaging, and practical content that helps you master your passion.

Focal Press and you.

Bound to create.

We'd love to hear how we've helped
you create. Share your experience:
www.focalpress.com/boundtocreate

Contents

Contents

ix

Contents

Contents

A Bit About Me

I began my career as a lighting designer and programmer working in the early 1990s with some of the top names in the country music industry including Kathy Mattea, Michelle Wright, Suzie Bogguss, Pam Tillis, Glen Campbell, and The Mandrell Sisters (Barbara, Louise and Irlene). I left the concert and touring world however in 1994 to join the dynamic Sales Support Services team at High End Systems® (HES). While traveling the world for HES, I worked with a lot of designers and programmed many kinds of shows ranging from tradeshow booths, concerts, festivals, and TV shows, to the opening ceremonies of the 2000 Summer Olympics in Sydney. And as the Control Systems Training Manager for HES, I also oversaw the development of training courses for all of HES's control systems products including Status Cue®, Wholehog® 2 and III, and Catalyst® while also consulting with and developing curriculums for colleges and universities including Liverpool Institute for Performing Arts (LIPA) and Full Sail University.

Since leaving HES in the mid-2000s, I briefly returned to the freelance world in live music and television, and then I landed in Las Vegas to work for Production Resource Group® (PRG) as a product specialist for practically any lighting console and media server that someone can rent or own including PRG's proprietary Mbox® Designer. On a daily basis I am challenged to offer technical support and expertise in all areas of lighting and video design and programming. I continue to speak at conferences such as LDI and to consult and train for numerous entities such as the International

Association of Theatrical Stage Employees (IATSE), hotels, theaters, and production staff because I am a fervent believer in sharing knowledge with those who seek it.

It was during my years at HES that I was introduced to the bleeding edge of lighting and video technology, the Catalyst Media Server. Being from a lighting background, I was not familiar with video equipment or terminology in any significant way, so I began a learning journey that has continued all the way until the present day. I have had a front row seat as two distinct divisions of our entertainment industry have continued to crossover and merge in exciting new ways. This is due, primarily, to the popularity of DMX controlled media servers among lighting designers and programmers, and today most major lighting manufacturers offer some type of DMX controlled media server for lighting professionals. All anyone has to do is watch a concert, an awards show, or a dancing or singing competition reality show to see a media server in action.

In 2006 I began writing a featured column for *Production Lights and Staging News* called "Video Digerati." This column has allowed me to delve deeply into this world in between lighting and video, discovering new technology, and meeting new people. This book is inspired by that research, and contains the fruits of all the time I have spent both looking up answers to questions I had, asking experts, and working in this business with technology experts and creatively gifted people like Richard Belliveau, Tim Grivas, Brad Schiller, Richard Bleasdale, Matthias Hinrichs, and others; the list is very long, too long to list here. To each and every one of the industry professionals that have shared a piece of their knowledge with me, I am very thankful and forever grateful. What I hope to achieve with this book is to pay that forward and help to demystify somewhat the media server for those lighting designers and programmers who are interested in learning more about this exciting and quickly evolving area of lighting but not sure where to start. So let's get started!

Vickie Claiborne, 2013.

Introduction

WHAT IS A MEDIA SERVER?

A media server allows a large library of media files to be quickly recalled and manipulated and then stored into a sequence, cuelist, or other type of playback system for use in a show. The true power of a media server is that it allows the real-time manipulation of attributes like play speed and play direction of a clip, layering of still images, masking, keystone correction, color, intensity, scale, rotation of the image along X, Y, and Z axis, and mapping an image to a 3D object. This is similar to the concept of using a non-linear editing program like the Adobe® After Effects® to add effects to a video clip but without having to wait while the clip is rendered each time something is added before viewing the composite results. Today's digital media servers give designers the ability to save these digitally layered results into a cue that can be recalled either through a user interface on the server, a separate control application, or via a lighting console.

Without a media server, the playback of video content is limited to exactly what is rendered. No live changes or manipulations are possible without sophisticated video equipment. Media servers, however, put that kind of control into the hands of the production designer, allowing more room for creativity over merely playing a fully rendered video clip.

While video engineers have used computers for the playback of video for many years, the use of media servers by lighting programmers is still a relatively young field. The development of automated lighting capable of projecting 'digital gobos' helped pave the way for the evolution of the DMX controlled media server while opening the door to new technology that allows video clips to be triggered via a lighting cue recorded on a lighting console. Digital lighting has changed the lighting industry forever.

Due to the popularity of media servers in recent years, practically every major lighting manufacturer sells a server today. As a result, there are many servers to choose from, too many to cover each and every one in this book. However, I have included a wide range of principles and knowledge that most lighting programmers use when working with media servers, so my goal for the scope of this book is to be broad enough that the information contained within can be applied in many applications.

CHAPTER 1

How Did We Get Here? A Brief Look at the Beginnings of Digital Lighting

When automated lighting first debuted, fixtures were extremely limited in the number of patterns that could fit in the unit. Manufacturers constantly pushed to develop fixtures with more gobos and effects in response to demand from lighting designers. However, the trade off as manufacturers developed new products was larger, heavier lighting fixtures with as many as three gobo wheels. But there is an upper limit to the size of a fixture you want to hang on a truss. These fixtures, while providing more than 20 patterns in some cases, simply took up more space in the rig. Other factors like price (some of these fixtures cost upwards of US$10,000 each) were also prohibitive. That kind of money for so few patterns was the inspiration that some major lighting manufacturers needed to find an effective way of creating a lighting fixture with a digital gobo library. The goal for those manufacturers eventually became a fixture that could have a virtually endless supply of images while enabling designers the freedom of selecting unique images instead of using stock patterns that may have been used on hundreds of other shows.

In the mid-1990s, Light & Sound Design (LSD) debuted a product called the Icon M (Medusa). When it came on the scene it was a revolutionary breakthrough in the lighting industry. While it only saw limited use and remained an in-house product due to reasons like the fixture's Digitial Light Processing (DLP®) micromirror technology (not used in today's digital lighting luminaires), low output, and its need for proprietary control, it did prove that the industry could create a fixture with a much larger library of digital images.

THE ICON M LUMINAIRE

LAMP SOURCE:	1200W MSR
BEAM ANGLE:	8-24° Zoom (100,000:1 DIGITAL ZOOM)**
IRIS:	DIGITAL**
STROBE:	DIGITAL**
COLOUR WHEEL:	CUSTOM
2ND COLOUR WHEEL:	NO
COLOUR MIXING:	PARAMETRIC COLOUR SYSTEM
EFFECTS WHEEL:	NO
FIXED GOBOS:	DIGITAL**
ROTATING GOBOS:	DIGITAL**
PRISM:	NO
REMOTE FOCUS:	YES
REMOTE LAMP STRIKE:	YES
HOT RESTRIKE:	NO
WEIGHT:	N/A
SIZE:	997 x 530 x 610MM
POWER CONSUMPTION:	N/A
8/16 BIT:	N/A
DMX CHANNELS:	ICON PROTOCOL ONLY

*PRELIMINARY RELEASE INFORMATION ONLY

** THE ICON M LUMINAIRE UTILIZES THE TEXAS INSTRUMENTS DIGITAL LIGHT PROCESSING (DLP) MICROMIRROR TECHNOLOGY. FEATURES INCLUDE 1,000 DIGITAL GOBOS AND 250 CUSTOM VECTOR IMAGES OR GRAYSCALE BITMAPS, EACH WITH INSTANT RANDOM ACCESS. IMAGES CAN BE SHAPED, CROPPED, SCALED, ROTATED, INDEXED, TILED, BLURRED, DIFFUSED, OVERLAID, ANIMATED, AND MORPHED. THE ICON M CONTAINS THE ENTIRE DHA GOBO CATALOGUE ONBOARD. DLP ENABLES DIGITAL DIMMING, IRIS, STROBE, AND ZOOM FUNCTIONS.

FIGURE 1.1
Icon M spec sheet.

High End Systems (HES) continued the research and development on solving the digital gobo problem, and in the late 1990s HES teamed up with hardware developers Wynne Willson-Gottelier (WWG) Ltd. and SAM Show Control software developer Richard Bleasdale to develop a prototype digital lighting product, code named Vertigo. In its earliest form, Bleasdale's control software (the foundation for today's Catalyst Media Server software) provided the source and control of the digital images while WWG's orbital projection head, attached to a large scale projector, provided the ability to pan and tilt the very bright source of light from mid to large size projectors (5 k to 18 k lumens) from a DMX lighting console. This prototype continued to evolve and eventually became Catalyst and the Catalyst™ Orbital Head.

FIGURE 1.2
Catalyst Orbital Head.

3

This was an important milestone because using Catalyst meant that the lighting programmer would have the ability to control digital images that could be fed to a projector, and the Orbital Head allowed the programmer the ability to aim the digital images anywhere on any surface while controlling the speed of the movement between focus locations as well as the keystone correction needed when projecting at angles other than 90 degrees. This breakthrough opened up the minds of everyone in the lighting industry, and video suddenly became a new aspect of the lighting programmer's world.

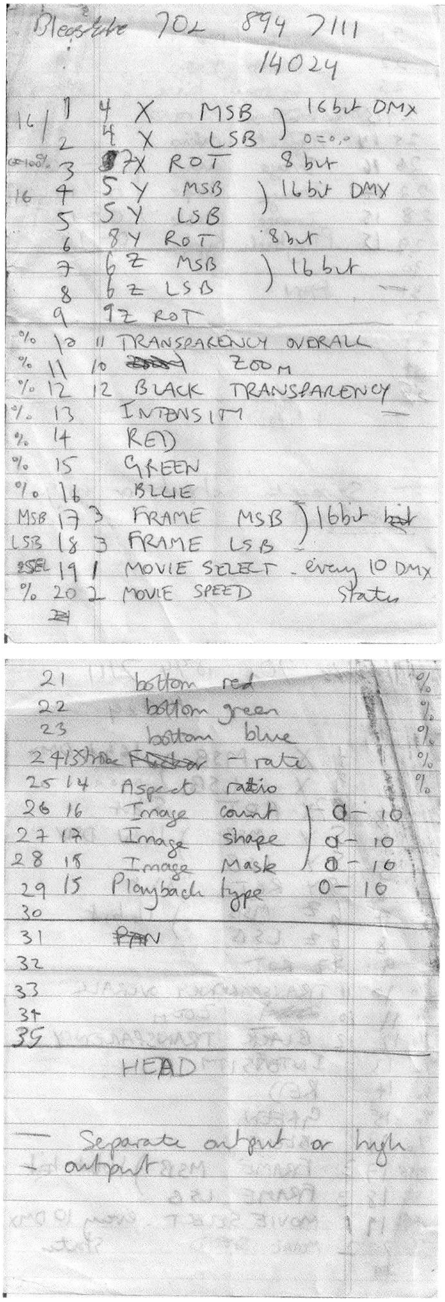
Bleastike 702 894 7111
14024
16 1 4 X MSB } 16bit DMX
2 4 X LSB 0=0,0
100% 3 7X ROT 8 bit
16 4 5 Y MSB } 16bit DMX
5 5 Y LSB
6 8 Y ROT 8bit
7 6 Z MSB } 16 bit
8 6 Z LSB
9 9 Z ROT
% 10 11 TRANSPARENCY OVERALL
% 11 10 ZOOM
% 12 12 BLACK TRANSPARENCY
% 13 INTENSITY
% 14 RED
% 15 GREEN
% 16 BLUE
MSB 17 3 FRAME MSB } 16bit
LSB 18 3 FRAME LSB
SEL 19 1 MOVIE SELECT - every 10 DMX
% 20 2 MOVIE SPEED Static

21 bottom red %
22 bottom green %
23 bottom blue %
24 13 - rate %
25 14 Aspect ratio %
26 16 Image count } 0 - 10
27 17 Image shape 0 - 10
28 18 Image Mask 0 - 10
29 15 Playback type 0 - 10
30
31 PAN
32
33
34
35
HEAD
— Separate output or high
+ output

FIGURE 1.3
Early Catalyst notes. *Source:* Courtesy of Brad Schiller.

CHAPTER 2

Why Do LDs Want to Control Video from a Lighting Console?

While video is an exciting world of creative visuals, the design and control of video has a distinctive set of criteria that has to be met in order to effectively manage the playback of a video. As such, there are many video engineers that do not agree that controlling video from a lighting console is a good thing. In fact, most video engineers have never touched a lighting console and do not truly understand how a channel with 256 bits can control their video. So they prefer to stick with their tried and true methods of control. And that's ok! But for the rest of us adventurers (aka lighting programmers) who want to cross over, using a lighting console is the least of the concerns. Here are some of the pros and cons typically heard when discussing using a lighting console for video control.

PROS

Lighting designers (LDs) in the past had to rely on separate personnel from a different discipline to execute video aspects of the show. Controlling a media server via DMX eliminates this problem and allows the operator to be able to playback video effects simultaneously in the same cue as other lighting fixtures are also being told to change colors, patterns, positions, etc. Also, designers who are familiar with current video equipment are always amazed at how easy it is to manipulate video images live, in real time, without re-rendering each change. Controlling video from a DMX console also enables the LD more input into the overall look and feel of the show, and the programmer working with both lighting and video is better able to balance levels between the lighting and video aspects, something which is generally very difficult to do when lighting is controlled from one location and video from another.

Positive points for controlling video from a lighting console:

1. *The lighting designer oversees the whole picture.* What this means is that the LD can create more cohesive visual looks that combine lighting and video, and the execution of the cues will be tighter as well.
2. *Fewer hands in the mix.* If the LD is calling the shots on how a video is played, there are fewer opportunities for missed cues or wrong videos at the wrong time.
3. *Simplification of control.* Most media servers today can handle video camera inputs, switching, and audio output, for example. And if less video gear is needed during the show, fewer operators will be needed as well.
4. *Video clips can be manipulated in real time.* This is a very important concept. Why? Because a pre-rendered video clip is what it is. When a video engineer plays it back using a standard video mixer, the video clip will play back exactly as it was rendered. Not so with a media server. The pre-rendered video clip is merely a suggestion of what the final composited image can be. A media server allows for real-time manipulation of video clips while being controlled from the lighting console. This means a virtually endless number of

visual creations are possible because a piece of content can be affected via visual effects, color effects, size effects, etc, available both in the media server and in the lighting console.

FIGURE 2.1
FOH lighting and video control.

NOW FOR THE CONS

Currently there are many choices for professional video gear available in the market, each with its own merits. Therefore, it can be difficult for the lighting designer to be in complete control of all of the video aspects used in a show. The video industry tends to favor routing the media server through a switcher so it becomes one of the sources instead of the media server handling the switching between video devices. But with the introduction into media servers of features like live camera inputs, audio inputs, and serial device control, some technically savvy lighting programmers (who are somewhat video savvy as well) are undertaking the complete integration of video control from their lighting consoles and having great success.

Negative points against controlling video from a lighting console:

1. *The limitations of the technology.* Video equipment is highly specialized and therefore has been optimized to handle all of the tasks of video playback. Media servers and lighting consoles are digital solutions to video playback and are somewhat limited in areas including the number of video outputs, speed of accessing media, quality of output, and previewing a piece of video content. Best to know the limitations so there are no surprises on show site.

2. *Less time for a complete design of both elements.* If an LD's time is split between lighting and video for a performer like a big pop star, for instance, then he/she will likely not have much quality time to completely develop the cues for both. So it might be best in some cases to separate the responsibilities of video from lighting and return it to the video team.

3. *The workload for a single programmer to manage two time-consuming elements can be overwhelming.* If one programmer is programming both lighting and video, then both may not be as thoroughly programmed and tight as they would be if the jobs were divided between two people. Therefore, it is very common on jobs where a media server(s) is being used to separate them out to a second lighting console and have a second programmer to focus strictly on the media servers.

The bottom line for deciding when to use a media server or when to stay out of video world entirely is simple: the quality of the production cannot be allowed to suffer. So, remember, just because you can control video from a lighting desk or directly from a media server does not mean you should. Considering the workload ahead of time will mean a smoother show all around.

8

CHAPTER 3

Convergence and the Role of the Lighting Programmer

As lighting consoles continue to be upgraded with new features for the integration of video, the job of the programmer gets more complex. The development of the digital media server has unlocked a world of possibilities for designers and allowed video to be more easily integrated into a wider range of shows. This is further solidified by the continual development of new lighting/video technology (aka digital lighting). So it seems probable that at some point in a lighting programmer's career, he/she will find him/herself programming a media server.

Programming with Wholehog 3 and Catalyst (2005)

Programming with grandMA2®, Ai® & DL.3® (2012)

FIGURE 3.1
Making the magic happen.

THE RESPONSIBILITIES OF THE MEDIA SERVER PROGRAMMER

Lighting programmers are primarily responsible for mood, and mood is created through the use of movement, color, intensity, and texture. Although, in most cases an artist's image is not identified with a specific lighting cue or color; instead, the media server programmer is directly involved with conveying the artist's 'image' and/or a visual message. Consequently, it is typical for the artist and/or artist's management to be very hands on when it comes to any video content used in the show.

On a show utilizing a media server, the role of lighting programmer has changed significantly. For example, the programmer is not only responsible for making sure that the content used in the show meets the client's expectations, he/she may also be somewhat responsible for the technical aspects of how the video will be presented through factors like screen reflectivity, size and placement, and content preparation and formatting. The lighting programmer who has a general working knowledge of these types of video elements will have an advantage over those who do not in these situations, and he/she can help to minimize the number of technical errors in the video playback.[1]

This leads us to a frequently asked question: Are video engineers in danger of being replaced by lighting programmers? My definitive answer is: on some gigs, yes, on some gigs no. How is that for non-committal? In all seriousness, the answer depends upon several factors, including:

1. Budget
2. Scale of show
3. Programming and organizational abilities of the lighting programmer
4. Trust in the lighting programmer to be able to handle the visual aspects of the production.

DMX controlled Digital Media Servers definitely seem to be here to stay. Today, most major lighting manufacturers either already sell a media server or are developing one. As a result, lighting designers and/or visual designers now have many choices for controlling the visual aspects of the show from one control source. Will that lead to a reduction in video technicians on shows? Not likely. Video technicians are an essential part of the equation. On shows where a media server is used, video technicians are still needed to properly set up and maintain the projectors, Light Emitting Diode (LED) walls, cameras, teleprompter, etc. During rehearsals and shows, the lighting programmer is tied to the console and is not easily able to attend to problems with equipment when they arise, so video technicians are absolutely necessary in order to troubleshoot those problems and ensure a smooth performance. So I believe the sandbox is big enough for everyone; and luckily the sandbox keeps getting bigger as well, creating more opportunities for programmers and video technicians alike.

11

CHAPTER 4

Getting Familiar with Hardware

There are a few hardware options to consider when selecting a media server for a show. While there are all kinds of video equipment designed for specific applications, the advantage of using a media server is its flexibility and concise package. When one piece of equipment can perform multiple tasks, it can save time, money, and energy spent rounding up the multitude of gear and manpower required to achieve the same results as traditional video methods.

It is helpful to be familiar with the components of a server system so that you have a clear understanding of what the server is capable of delivering in terms of performance and reliability. In this chapter we will take a look at all of the basic elements of a system including computer hardware and video cable connectors.

PARTS OF A MEDIA SERVER

1. *Graphics card*

   The graphics card of a media server outputs the video signal being generated by the server to the projection devices. There are far too many graphics cards on the market today to list them all here, but generally most cards in servers will utilize one of three types of video connections: Video

Graphics Array (VGA), Digital Visual Interface (DVI), and/ or High-Definition Multimedia Interface (HDMI).

FIGURE 4.1
NVidia® graphics card.

2. *Video capture card*

Video capture cards are typically used to capture external video sources onto the internal hard drive of a computer. This captured media can then be imported into content creation software applications or manipulated via special capturing software for playback. Capture cards may also be used to integrate a live video input feed from a source (instead of hard drive based content) when the video input channel of a media server (if available) is enabled from the lighting console or user interface. Video capture cards may be either internal or external: internal capture cards may be installed into a Peripheral Component Interconnect (PCI) or PCI Express slot on the computer's motherboard, while external cards may be attached via Universal Serial Bus (USB).[2] Most capture cards accept digital video input via High-Definition Serial Digital Interface (HD-SDI), Serial Digital Interface (SDI), Firewire, S-Video, Component, and/or Composite.

FIGURE 4.2
Blackmagic® video capture card.

3. *Hard drives*

The application and content storage drives play a very important role in the overall performance of a media server. There are several types available so it is important to understand the features of each type in order to understand how a media server is designed.

- *SATA* (acronym for Serial ATA): An example of SATA hardware specs used is 500 GB 7,200 rpm. SATA drives are commonly used as the boot/application drive in media servers.
- *RAID* (acronym for Redundant Array of Independent Disks): RAID arrays combine multiple disk drives into a single drive then distribute data among them, resulting in better performance. RAID arrays are commonly used for the storage of content in media servers.
- *SSD* (acronym for Solid State Drive): SSDs have no moving parts, making them resistant to shock and vibrations and ideal for use in media servers mounted in touring racks. Start up time for an SSD is extremely fast due to its lack of a spinning disc, and it is capable of accessing data at very high

15

speeds. SSDs are more expensive than traditional high-density hard drives (HDD), and this is the main factor that limits their use in the media server market currently.

- *SCSI* (aka SCUZZY): acronym for Small Computer System Interface. Prior to the faster (10,000 rpm) speeds of SATA technology, SCSI was typically preferred for most media servers (e.g. Catalyst). However, as technology keeps changing, advancements in hardware mean SCSI drives are not commonly found in media servers.

MAC VERSUS PC

The ongoing debate of "Mac or PC" comes to mind when discussing a media server. Digital media servers range in size, features, and even software platforms. There are many factors that drive a manufacturer to choose one platform over another. For instance, if you ask someone what a Mac® is known for, the typical answer will be stability and exceptional graphics. Both Catalyst (Richard Bleasdale) and Mbox Designer (PRG) are based on this platform for these reasons as well as a few others. PRG's R&D team originally chose the Mac platform for its Virtuoso® lighting console because of integrated support for multiple monitors and 3D rendering from the operating system (OS) at the time. When PRG and Vari-Lite Production Services (VLPS) merged a few years ago, two prior models of media servers, the Mbox and the EX-1® were combined to make the present day Mbox Designer. However, the R&D team chose to continue on the Mac platform even though the EX-1 was a PC based application because of its extensive experience in Mac development.

Manufacturers of PC based servers like Axon® (High End Systems), Hippotizer™ (Green Hippo®), and Maxedia™ (Martin®) have a common theme behind their choice of

PC over Mac: hardware options, and more specifically, the ability to design a purpose built server. Also, many people just simply prefer the DirectX™ technology over the Mac OpenGL® platform for performance reasons. Other media servers like ArKaos® MediaMaster™ Pro were co-developed from the beginning on both platforms primarily to increase the market of potential buyers.

What does this mean to you? While Macs are known to be very user friendly, secure, and stable, upgradeability is limited and the OS cannot be used on any other hardware than a Mac. PCs, on the other hand, can be purpose built and have unlimited upgradeability via graphics cards, Random Access Memory (RAM), and other hardware. However, certain OS versions can be unreliable and are more susceptible to viruses than Macs. Things to consider when choosing one platform over another are the media server's feature set, the type of application, the number of video outputs, and the programmer's comfort level with one or the other OS. In my opinion, it is best to pick the one that has the feature set you need rather than just using the one that the rental shop has available; not all media servers have the same features.[3]

HOW DOES A MEDIA SERVER CONNECT TO A CONSOLE?

DMX (Digital MultipleX) controlled media servers allow for the ability to control video via a DMX signal. For the communication between console and server to happen, the server will likely be connected to the console via a hardware interface or directly via Ethernet, and the control signal will either be DMX (5-pinXLR) or DMX over Ethernet (e.g. Art-Net™). If a hardware interface is configured into the media server, it will usually feature a DMX input to connect to the lighting console as well as video signal outputs that connect to the display devices. Manufacturers like PRG

17

(Mbox Designer) create very clever interface modules (IO Module) that convert DMX to USB to control layers of a video signal, effects, cameras, and other features internally. Other media server manufacturers like Green Hippo choose to allow the lighting console to connect directly to the server via Ethernet; this simplifies the connection process and utilizes the server's internal hardware and software for control and communication.

FIGURE 4.3
Mbox IO module.

VIDEO ELEMENTS OF A SERVER

Outputs

Media servers differ in the number of video outputs available and what their purposes are. Typically, a server will have at least two video outputs, one of which can be assigned as a preview monitor for viewing the server's output locally at FOH if desired. However, if the server has a single video output card installed, this will prevent you from having any type of preview monitor.

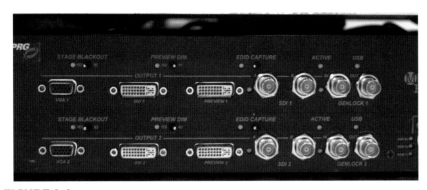

FIGURE 4.4
Close-up of video outputs on a server.

Many servers with dual video output cards also allow you the freedom and flexibility of controlling each output independently. If the server does have multiple outputs, there will be a setup mode for assigning the outputs and their functions within the application, and this must be configured before patching the server to a lighting console in order for the DMX personality to match.[4]

FIGURE 4.5
Catalyst video output management.

Signals and Cables

When you've taken on the task of programming a media server, you will be communicating closely with the video technician so there are a few technical details that you will need to discuss. Are you using SDI? DVI? Component? Here are a few brief descriptions to help determine those answers.

1. *VGA*

   VGA stands for Video Graphics Array, and it was the most common format found on computer graphics cards prior to DVI. Using a 15-pin connector, VGA carries analog component RGBHV (Red, Green, Blue, Horizontal, and Vertical) data for up to 5 ft/1.5 m reliably. Longer lengths may work, but the signal may not be reliable and therefore is usually not recommended.

   There are several resolutions in the VGA family including:

   - VGA 640 × 480
   - SVGA 800 × 600 (super video graphics array)
   - XGA 1024 × 768 (extended graphics array)
   - SXGA 1280 × 1024 (super extended graphics array)
   - WUXGA 1920 × 1200 (widescreen ultra extended graphics array)

2. *Component*

   A component video cable (also known as RGBHV or 5-wire BNC) carries five separate analog video signals and can be used for longer distances than VGA (100 ft and up).

3. *Composite*

   A composite video cable combines all five analog signals into one signal cable and can be used for longer distances than VGA (100 ft and up). Consumer rated composite cables typically use a connector known as an RCA connector whereas professional cables use a BNC connector.

FIGURE 4.6
(top) VGA, (left)
component, and (right)
composite cables.

4. *DVI*

DVI, which is an acronym for Digital Visual Interface, can carry an uncompressed digital video signal to a digital display device such as an LCD (Liquid Crystal Display) display or projector. It is capable of detecting the type of device it is connected to because it supports Extended Display Identification Data (EDID). EDID is the link between a computer graphics card and the display device and it provides a "handshake" between the devices. That same EDID information also tells the source device, such as a PC, to output at a specific resolution.

5. *Connectors*

There are three types of DVI cable connections: DVI-digital, DVI-analog, and DVI-integrated (digital and analog)

- DVI-D: digital to digital signal only (no analog)
- DVI-A: digital to analog signal (for use with VGA display devices)

21

- DVI-I: transmits digital or analog signals and can be used with both types of display devices. DVI-I will detect and choose the analog or digital portion of the interface depending on the type of display device that is connected.

6. *Pin configuration*

DVI cables come in a variety of pin configurations as well. You can spot a DVI-D cable easily by its lack of pins surrounding the flat blade, while a DVI-I cable has a flat blade that is surrounded by four pins; these pins are needed to carry the analog signal. Figure 4.7 gives an illustration of the pins and blade configurations of each of the types of DVI connectors.

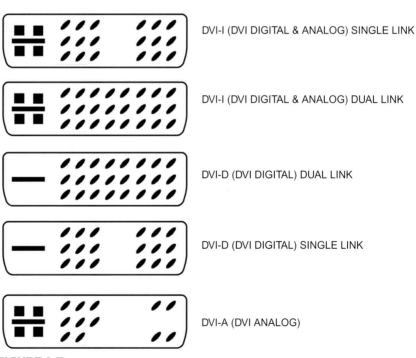

DVI-I (DVI DIGITAL & ANALOG) SINGLE LINK

DVI-I (DVI DIGITAL & ANALOG) DUAL LINK

DVI-D (DVI DIGITAL) DUAL LINK

DVI-D (DVI DIGITAL) SINGLE LINK

DVI-A (DVI ANALOG)

FIGURE 4.7
DVI pin configurations.

7. *Signal transmission*

Another aspect of a DVI cable is signal transmission. A DVI cable can be either single or dual link. The dual link DVI pins effectively double the power of transmission and provide an increase in speed and signal quality. Therefore, the dual link DVI cable is used for high resolution displays including 1600 × 1200 or 1920 × 1080. (See Figure 4.7 for an example of dual and single link connectors.)

8. *Cable length*

DVI is only recommended for cable lengths up to 16 ft/5 m. For longer distances, the use of a DVI booster is recommended to amplify the signal while eliminating potential signal degradation (artifacts, flickering, or blank screen). The potential for signal degradation over a longer digital cable due to data loss is more of a limitation for DVI cables than for analog cables.

When using DVI, there are a few important things to remember:

- *No hot swapping when using DVI cables!* If you need to unplug a DVI cable from the computer, then you have to power down the computer or use an EDID capture device (one type is the Gefen® DVI Detective) to hold the signal. Failure to do this properly will result in the screens being refreshed and possibly causing the output to automatically be switched to another available connected device.
- *Do not use DVI to VGA adapters between two digital devices* or you will end up with analog signal; use a DVI-D cable!
- *Use short cable lengths up to a maximum of 16 ft/5 m.* If a longer length is needed, you can use DVI boosters or a fiber convertor and transmit over fiber optic cables.[5]

9. *SDI*

SDI, which is short for Serial Digital Interface, is the format and cable of choice when it comes to HD and/or broadcast applications. SDI can transmit both standard-definition (SD) and High-Definition (HD)

23

signals up to 1080p and 1080i. And SDI cables can be used to transmit HD signal up to 300 ft/92 m or an SD signal up to 1,000 ft/308 m making them very practical for most applications.

FIGURE 4.8
SDI cable.

10. *HDMI*

HDMI is an acronym for High-Definition Multimedia Interface. This popular cable type is quickly becoming the standard in the consumer video market because it carries both audio and video signals, and it offers encryption protection on digital content. And a big advantage for using HDMI in show situations over VGA and DVI is longer signal cable lengths (up to 49 ft/15 m with high quality cables).

FIGURE 4.9
HDMI cable.

11. *BNC connector*

BNC connectors are commonly found on professional rated video coaxial cables, including composite, component, and SDI cables. The distinct connector locks into place when rotated, making the connection secure.

FIGURE 4.10
BNC connector.

Whether it is internal hardware or external cables, knowing what each of the parts are and what their functions are can greatly improve the performance of the entire system.

CHAPTER 5

What Does that Piece of Equipment Do?

In this chapter we will take a look at some of the types of products commonly used with media servers. It is almost a given that you will encounter most, if not all, of these at one time or another while working with media servers. Knowing a little about each of them will make your life a lot easier:

- LED wall
- Projector
- Video scaler
- Scan converter
- Video switcher
- VDA
- ImagePro HD

LED WALL

Rigid LED video panels come in a wide range of resolutions ranging from 4 mm to 100 mm+ and are available from many companies including Martin, Elation, PRG-Nocturne, and Winvision. LEDs have also found their way into soft goods, and LED curtains can now be found in resolutions ranging from 18 mm to 100 mm, available from companies like PixelFLEX® and Mainlight.

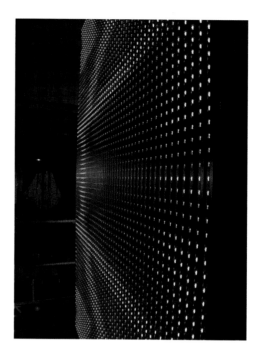

FIGURE 5.1
Martin LC™ 2140 LED panels.

LED screens, panels, and displays, whether soft or rigid, generally require a processor for operation. The processor's main purpose is not only to receive the incoming video signal that will be displayed, but also to manage the distribution of that signal out to the screens and/or tiles in the correct configuration. Companies like Barco have been making these types of LED processors for many years and they are very useful for scaling an image, positioning an image across multiple outputs, and for applying effects like chroma-keying or alpha-keying.

PROJECTOR

Projector technology continually advances to feature higher resolutions, brighter outputs, and smaller housings and is used in a wide range of live entertainment applications ranging from corporate events and trade shows to retail stores and concerts. Some terminology pertaining to projectors include:

- *Lumens*: projector brightness is rated in lumens, and units will typically be referred to by their output, as in 20 k (20,000 lumens) or 5 k (5,000 lumens).
- *DLP (Digital Light Processing)*: in very general terms, a DLP projector creates an image via the reflection of light off of tiny micromirrors embedded on a semiconductor chip inside its optics train.
- *LCD (Liquid Crystal Display)*: LCD projectors create an image by first passing light through a prism to separate the red, green, and blue components onto panels. Then, by applying an electronic charge to a layer of liquid crystal between each panel, an image will be formed and recombined before passing through the lens. As a result of this process, LCD projectors are typically able to display more saturated colors and sharper images than DLP projectors.
- *Chip set*: DLP projectors are referred to as single chip or 3-chip DLP, and while the distinction does refer to the number of chips present in the system, it is also a good indication as to the type of color production system that the projector may have, i.e. color wheel or separation by prism.
- *Lens size*: determining the correct lens size is a crucial part of selecting the right gear for the job. The wrong lens can mean disaster on site.

VIDEO SCALER

A video scaler is used to process an image in one resolution and resize it to a completely different resolution. A word of caution however, when scaling an image: an image that actually contains 800 × 600 pixels of information will look better than an image with 640 × 480 pixels of information scaled up

29

to a resolution of 800 × 600 pixels in the display. The Gefen®
HDSDI to DVI scaler is an example of this type of product.

SCAN CONVERTER

What does a scan converter do? In simple terms, it converts
a video signal from one format to another (e.g. from DVI to
SDI). The scan converter also has the ability to capture the
incoming signal and transmit it out again at a different scan-
rate (e.g. 25 Hz to 30 Hz).

All in One

The Barco® ImagePRO® HD is an example of a scan converter
as well as a video scaler and switcher. It is commonly referred
to as the "swiss army knife" of video tools because it can literally take in just about any video signal, convert it to another,
and send it back out. This flexibility makes it incredibly useful
in situations where there may be different signals and/or connectors that need to be connected. I learned early on just how
helpful this tool can be, so now I always add one of these to
an order when using a media server just in case.

FIGURE 5.2
Barco ImagePRO HD.

VIDEO SWITCHER

Video switchers feature multiple inputs and outputs and
they allow flexible routing of video and audio signals. Unless

combined with a scan converter, the switcher will not typically convert an incoming signal to another type of signal for output, so it is important to know exactly what type of signal you are using and what the gear on the show is so that you can plan accordingly. The Barco® Encore® Presentation Switcher and the Extron® SW4 AR switcher are examples of professional video switchers commonly used by video engineers.

FIGURE 5.3
Extron® SW4 AR HV video switcher.

31

VDA

A VDA (video distribution amplifier) does two things, both of which are in the name: it receives a video signal, boosts it, and then distributes the signal to multiple outputs.

FIGURE 5.4
VDA 2 × 1.

While each of these types of equipment perform very specific functions, all or some of them may not be necessary in every situation. Resolution, number of display devices, and, as always, budget will need to be factored in so that you can plan for the most effective video control solution possible. And if your media server can perform some of these functions without the need for additional gear, then by all means use it if you can but only if it does not make life too complicated for yourself and others. It is likely that you may find yourself in a situation on a corporate show where you know the media server you are working with can handle a specific task like switching cameras or playing back audio with a video, but because the video or audio engineer on the same show is already equipped or prepared to handle the task, it may simplify the situation to leave it to those technicians and focus on the tasks you have on your own plate.

CHAPTER 6

Programming a Media Server from a Lighting Console

Playing back clips from a media server can be accomplished in a variety of ways, and will vary slightly between manufacturers. Some allow the lighting programmer to create and store scenes on the media server itself and then to trigger those presets from the lighting console; other media servers allow the programmer direct access to its attributes from a lighting console via DMX channels, and the programmer records the looks directly into cues on the console. In this chapter we take a closer look at all the methods of using DMX to control a media server.

ASSIGNING DMX ADDRESSES

The method for assigning DMX addresses will be determined by the server (or quite possibly a mode on the server), and this varies greatly between server types. Generally speaking, in order for it to be controlled via DMX, the server in some way will have a convention to allow its individual channels and/or pre-recorded presets to be controlled via a DMX console. Regardless of how the address is set, once the starting channel has been determined and assigned to the server, the order of the DMX channels in the server's DMX mapping will determine which channel on the lighting console accesses which parameter. This channel mapping is what we call the DMX protocol, and all lighting console manufacturers use this mapping to create fixture personalities for their consoles.

ACCESSING MEDIA FROM A LIGHTING CONSOLE

In most media editing applications, the concept of the *layer* is a crucial element to how an image is created; this is also true for playing back content on most media servers. On servers such as Hippotizer, Catalyst, and Axon, video content is directly accessed via a layer; therefore, the programmer begins programming with a server by selecting a layer via a fixture number or channel number that you assign during patching (depending on the console of choice).

Once selected, each layer, much like a lighting fixture, has an **intensity** control. This means that in order to see any output from the layer, its intensity must be assigned to a value greater than 0 (i.e. full). This convention works well from a lighting console perspective; the programmer simply interacts with the layers as if they were lighting fixtures. The main differences are simply in how the parameters of the layer (the fixture) are labeled and what they actually control. Instead of channels for **Gobo**, you may select images from channels labeled **Media Library** and **Media File**; instead of **Zoom**, you may use a channel labeled **X** and/or **Y scale**. There are many similarities between fixtures and layers but essentially the essence of programming with a media server is that each layer is a fixture with a certain number of channels, and any DMX console treats those layers the same way by sending out a DMX value to playback specific content and effects.

Across the range of media servers there can be varying numbers of possible layers (3, 6, and 12 are common examples). Each layer is independent and can be manipulated with completely different effects and content than other layers. Because of this, layers also usually have a priority. This means that when a clip is playing on Layer 1, if a second layer is added, it will block the output from the first layer so that it is no longer visible in the output. On many servers Layer 1 has the lowest priority, with higher priority given to higher numbered layers. What that means simply is that you cannot see through to a layer with a lower priority by default without using some visual effects.[6]

Most servers have a specific location where content is located. Typically any digital content stored on the server will need to be organized in such a way that the media server application recognizes the content as a legitimate file and allows access to that file from within the application. In the examples of Axon, Mbox Designer, Catalyst, and MediaMaster Pro, content will need to be stored into folders numbered between 0 and 255. Why is this numbering scheme used? Each of these content folders is mapped to a DMX value between 0 and 255 on a specific channel in the protocol. Inside each of those 256 folders is where the individual pieces of content are stored, up to 256 pieces per folder. Again, in the above media server examples, the individual files also need to be numbered between 0 and 255, and all of these values are mapped to a second specific DMX channel. Then, the programmer chooses a piece of content for display by selecting a media folder using Channel X, and then selecting a file within that folder using Channel Y.

	ArKaos Layer Full 1.0					
	Channel	Ranges	Snap/Instant	Default Value	Locate Value	Category
1	DIMMER	0-100%	NO	0	255	DIMMER
2	VISUAL LIBRARY	0 USER FOLDER 0	YES	0	0	BEAM
		1 USER FOLDER 1				
		...				
		239 USER FOLDER 239				
		240 GENERATORS				
		242 AUDIO FLASH				
		250 FLASH TEXTS 1				
		251 FLASH TEXTS 2				
		252 FLASH TEXTS 3				
		253 FLASH TEXTS 4				
		254 CAMERAS				
		255 MASKS				
3	FILE	0 PREV. LAYER	YES	0	1	BEAM
		1-255 FILE 1-255				
4	EFFECT LIBRARY	0-15 3D PRESETS	YES	0	0	BEAM
		16-31 COLOR PRESETS				
		32-47 BLUE PRESETS				
		48-63 SPLIT PRESETS				
		64-79 ARTISTIC PRESETS				
		80-95 3D (CUSTOM)				
		96-111 COLOR (CUSTOM)				
		112-127 BLUR (CUSTOM)				

FIGURE 6.1
MediaMaster Pro DMX protocol sample.

Selecting a piece of digital content is only the beginning of the fun. Once a piece of media has been selected to play, that piece of content can be manipulated in a virtually endless number of ways, very much in the same way a picture or video can be manipulated in a video compositing application. For instance, some of the typical layer attributes in media servers include:

- X, Y, Z positioning
- X, Y, Z scale
- X, Y, Z rotation
- Mask
- Play speed, direction, mode
- Intensity
- CMY color mixing

- Keystone control
- Brightness
- Contrast
- Audio, sound level
- In frame/out frame control
- Visual effects, i.e. tiling, alpha channel masking, visual distortions including posterizing, inverting, ripple, waves
- Camera input enable/disable.

If using an automated digital lighting fixture (e.g. DL.3®), additional fixture personalities that include controls for pan, tilt, shutter, and projector menu controls may be required.

DMX DEFAULT VALUES

In the DMX protocol created by the manufacturer, a default value will be determined for each DMX control channel of the media server. This default value is typically 0 or 100 for attributes like intensity or RGB (Red, Green, Blue); for attributes like pan, tilt, or zoom, the defaults may be any value. The default value for a channel is important because it is the value at which the fixture is considered to be 'at rest,' or as some call it 'home.' These values will be output from the DMX console at all times when there are no active DMX values from a cue present. It is possible on most consoles today to edit the default values if adjustments are necessary, and they also can persist from cue to cue when using a lighting console with a tracking feature. When programming, it is important to pay attention to all values of a layer, including default values, so that when you play back the cue, you get the desired look that you expect.

DMX CONTROL CHANNELS PER LAYER

The number of channels per layer can vary based on the desired programming mode (e.g. reduced, standard, or expanded). Most media servers offer modes for different control options, possibly including:

- Direct access to each control attribute of the software
- Programming onboard the media server, then using a greatly reduced number of channels to trigger the look from a DMX console via a channel value.

FIXTURE PERSONALITY

The mapping of DMX channels for a media server is created in much the same way as for an automated lighting fixture. The manufacturer of the server maps specific attribute functions to specific DMX channels, and then that channel map is supplied to the software engineers of all lighting consoles. Those engineers generate a profile (sometimes referred to as a personality) based on that DMX channel map and then that profile gets added into the console's profile library.

FIGURE 6.2
grandMA2 patch window showing manufacturer's list with profiles.

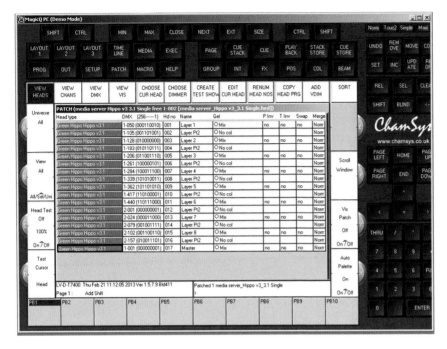

FIGURE 6.3
ChamSys® MagicQ™ Patch Window showing manufacturer's list with profiles.

PROGRAMMING WITH A PERSONALITY

How a personality for a digital lighting fixture or media server is written and displayed on the console has a tremendous impact on the performance of the lighting programmer. Attributes (the features) of the media server will typically be grouped into basic categories with other similar attributes. Accessing the category of color attributes, for example, may be as simple as selecting the **color** button (or menu) on the console and then all of the related color attributes will be mapped to the console's encoder wheels or other attribute control handles.

Another aspect of how a fixture's personality can impact programming is if DMX values are displayed in percentages instead of direct DMX values. If the encoder wheel that

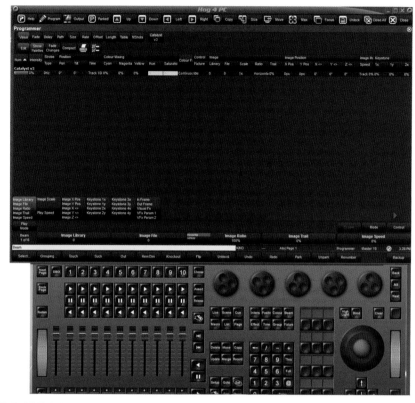

FIGURE 6.4
Hog®4PC encoders showing personality labeling.

is used to access the control channel for video files is set to 8-bit resolution, then it will likely skip a few values (which correspond to separate files) between each rotation of the wheel unless the wheel's resolution is set to FINE mode (16-bit resolution). Therefore, it is important to familiarize yourself with how a fixture's attributes are mapped on a lighting console and to make adjustments accordingly where possible (some consoles have a preference setting that allows the direct DMX values to be displayed as well as settings for 8-bit/16-bit resolution, aka FINE mode)

Some consoles feature a type of direct access toolbar or menu that allows access to individual attributes directly

FIGURE 6.5
MA™ onPC screen capture of Percentage, Hex and Real-World values.

(e.g. specific visual effects). For programmers using one of these consoles, it can be easier and faster to record palettes (also called presets) for a desired attribute. However, while a quick access toolbar can be handy for certain attributes, these toolbars do not provide access to the more detailed settings available for those features, i.e. rotation speed of an image or movie play speed and direction, for instance. So the toolbars may be somewhat convenient for a quick look, but not so much for more detailed adjustments.[7]

The creation of macros may also be necessary for certain features of a server, especially for some hardware related features such as **Server Shutdown** or **Graphic Engine Restart**. These types of control channels are typically never recorded into a lighting cue because you would not want to execute the shutdown command accidentally in the middle of your show. However, for convenience, the console programmer may

FIGURE 6.6
Hog4PC screen capture of Direct Access toolbar.

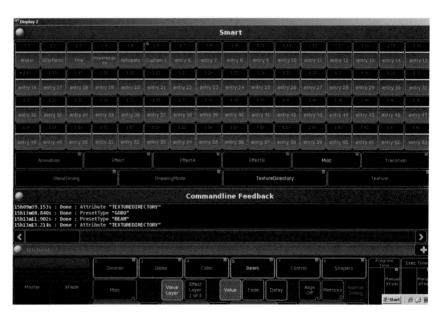

FIGURE 6.7
MA onPC screen capture of SMART window.

choose to make a keystroke macro to access the menu or control channel where the hardware control features are located, and then the programmer can manually execute that macro at any time desired.

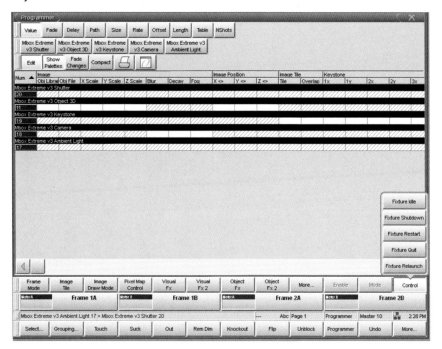

FIGURE 6.8
Hog®3PC screen capture of control channel settings.

CHALLENGES ARE JUST OPPORTUNITIES TO LEARN

Media servers are unique creative tools, and they can be both tremendously fun and complex at the same time. Taking the time to familiarize yourself with all of the attributes of a server that is new to you before you arrive onsite is truly the best way to get the most out of your programming experience. But be prepared for some hiccups and some head scratching moments too. All of these experiences make you smarter and better prepared for the next time!

CHAPTER 7

It's All About the Content

A media server's primary purpose is to play video content in a show. Therefore, the server has to have some digital content on it. Where does this content come from? Does the server have any preloaded (stock) content, or will you have to create and add custom content to the server? All digital content comes from one of the following sources:

- Stock content loaded on the server
- Content provided by client
- Content purchased from a content provider
- Content you create from scratch.

STOCK CONTENT

Media servers typically come loaded with a selection of licensed media content that can be used in any show. This content will already be properly formatted for use with the server and may include both still images and video clips. Also, because the stock content is not intended to be copied from the computer, most manufacturers have encryption on all stock content to prevent the misuse of its legally purchased content.

OBTAINING FROM CLIENT AND/OR PURCHASING CONTENT

If content is acquired either from the client or purchased from a content provider such as Artbeats® or Digital Juice™, it will need to be properly formatted according to the server's recommendations. This means, of course, that you should try really hard to get it from the client or provider well before the day of the show because every media server has a specific formatting requirement for digital media, and it can take some time to properly re-format a piece of content.

REAL-WORLD APPLICATIONS

These scenarios are inevitable for the media server programmer:

- The show you are programming will be using content created by a corporate graphics arts team, but the team is unfamiliar with the specifications required by the media server you are using.
- During rehearsals, the production manager of the show hands you an image of one of the corporate VIPs and wants to use it in the awards ceremony.

In both of these all-too-frequent scenarios where you are handed a CD, DVD, or USB drive containing miscellaneous content and told to use something on it in the show, the first thing that needs to happen is to ask if permission has been given to use the content. Once the license has been confirmed, the next step is to examine the content for its usability.

GARBAGE IN, GARBAGE OUT

Remember this rule: Garbage in, garbage out. What does that mean exactly? The media server can only display the content at the same quality it was created. If poorly rendered content is loaded on the server, then poorly rendered content will be what is output by the server.

Some common things to avoid using are low-resolution images, movies that are improperly formatted, and/or videos downloaded from social media sites. These types of low-resolution images are difficult to scale up without becoming visibly distorted and pixelated, and the results likely will not be usable or attractive. Knowing a bit about the properties of a piece of digital content may help save you some valuable time because you will avoid wasting time trying to improve something that cannot be improved.

My rule on this is simple: never use a piece of content in a show situation that has not been viewed and optimized for performance. Why? Because, as the media server programmer, it is my responsibility to ensure the maximum playback performance of all the images used in the show. It is always best not to use content that makes the system (and you) look unprofessional.

CREATING YOUR OWN CONTENT

When purchasing content is not an option or it simply does not exist, then creating it from scratch will be necessary. The first place to start is to identify what you need. Question #1 is usually, "What kind of content needs to be created?" Then, question #2 follows shortly thereafter, "Will it be still images, video clips, digital animations and/or 3D objects?" Once you have a few answers to these basic questions, you can begin to form a plan.

There are many important factors in the creation process that have direct impact on the playback performance of a piece of content. They include:

- Image resolution
- Image compression
- Format
- Frame rate.

IMAGE RESOLUTION

When an image is created, it will have a specific resolution (e.g. a specific number of pixels per inch/centimeter). What is a pixel? A pixel is one dot representing a single bit of information. Therefore, image resolution refers to the number of pixels in an image, or in simpler terms, it refers to how much information is included in the image. Resolution is sometimes identified by the width and height of the image as well as the total number of pixels in the image. For example, an image that is 2,048 pixels wide and 1,536 pixels high contains (multiply 2,048 w × 1,536 h) 3,145,728 pixels (or 3.1 megapixels). So the image can be referred to as a 3.1 megapixel image.

Changing the size of an image involves redistributing the available pixels across the designated space. If an image is made larger then the size of each pixel must be increased—consequently, the image will have fewer pixels per inch/centimeter (lower resolution). On the other hand, if an image is made smaller the size of each pixel must be decreased and the image will have more pixels per inch/centimeter (higher resolution).

48

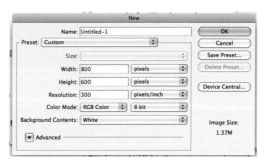

FIGURE 7.1
Settings for image width, height, and resolution.

DISPLAY RESOLUTION

When displaying an image on a monitor, the screen size determines the size of the image. Since there are a fixed number of pixels on a screen, if you're going to display an 800 × 600 image on a screen, then the number of pixels across the image will always be 800 but depending on the screen size, the pixels will be closer or farther apart.

The number of pixels from top to bottom (the height of the image on the monitor) is described as the number of lines, and the area of horizontal lines on the display is called the raster. Using Figure 7.2 as an example, there would be 600 pixel rows (lines) vertically when the image is displayed in that raster. If the resolution of the monitor changes, the image will still be displayed across 600 lines of the screen but it may appear larger or smaller because the lines are closer together or farther apart.

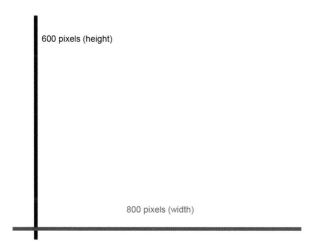

FIGURE 7.2
Illustration showing 800 × 600 resolution.

IMAGE RESOLUTION ON LED WALLS

When the output display device is an LED wall, how will the image be affected? This will depend greatly on how close the LEDs are positioned in the wall. The distance between adjacent pixels is called the *pitch*. It is usually measured in millimeters and the smaller the pitch size, the better the image looks. In other words, the closer the pixels, the better the resolution. Pixel pitches in LED panels typically range from 2 mm up to 100 mm and panels come in all shapes and sizes.[8]

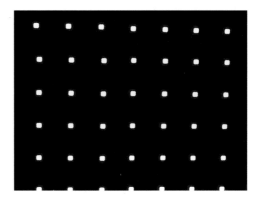

FIGURE 7.3
LED pixel pitch.

IMAGE COMPRESSION

A very important element of any piece of content is its compression setting. The quality of the image can also be manipulated via *compression*. An uncompressed image is saved in a file format that does not compress the pixels in the image at all. The downsides of an uncompressed image are that it not only takes up more space on the hard drive, it makes the processor in the media server work a little harder while displaying it, especially if the image is being played back along with other uncompressed images. If you want to reduce the *file size* (number of bytes required to save the image), then a compression format, referred to as a *codec*, can be selected when saving the file that may improve playback performance.

As a lighting programmer, the term *codec* may be foreign to you. However, it is a very important term to understand because it affects the content's playback performance more than any other single factor of content creation. A codec (an acronym for COmpressor-DECompressor or COder-DECoder) encodes a signal for transmission, storage, or encryption and then decodes it for viewing or editing.

Media servers typically require compression of a video signal in order to speed up the rate of data being processed and transferred. While signal compression allows higher data rates, it also has its drawbacks, not the least of which is how it potentially alters the video image. Due to this delicate balance between the quality of the video and the complexity of the encoding and decoding algorithms, among other factors, there are hundreds of codecs available for video signal compression and decompression that alter the image in different ways, in attempts to minimize the damage. Therefore, knowing the recommended codec for your server is imperative.[9]

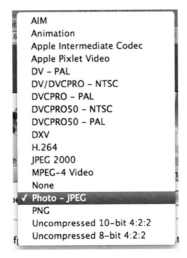

FIGURE 7.4
Final Cut Pro® codec list.

To illustrate the impact of using one codec over another let's take a look at this comparison between the DV-NTSC and Photo-JPEG codecs. Photo-JPEG preserves color information better than DV-NTSC; however, it is not as tightly compressed as DV-NTSC so it is also much slower. The DV-NTSC codec can be decoded much faster than the Photo-JPEG codec because of its compression ratio. Essentially this means that you may not be able to playback four layers of clips encoded with Photo-JPEG codec at same time without affecting frame rates. Playing four layers of DV-NTSC encoded clips would likely result in smoother playback performance and fewer dropped frames.

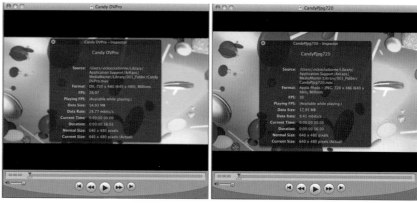

FIGURE 7.5
QuickTime® Pro DV and PJpeg codecs.

FORMAT

Still image formats that are commonly used in media servers include:

- PNG
- TIFF
- JPG
- BMP.

TIFF or BMP files are two examples of formats that do not compress the image. At the opposite end of the spectrum, if desired, images can be stored as a JPEG (acronym for Joint Photographic Experts Group), and the amount of compression you want can be selected before saving the image.

Common video formats recommended by many media servers include:

- Quicktime (.mov)
- AVI (.avi)
- MPEG (mpeg 4, .mp2, .mpg).

There are too many other formats to list here, so it is always recommended to check the server's documentation for the recommended format and settings required.

FRAME RATE

A video clip differs from a still image in that it contains information for multiple images that, when played back in order, produce a moving image. In simple terms, that information is organized into a set of all the pixels that correspond to a single point in time. This pixel set is called a *frame*. Basically, a frame is the same as a still picture, but the video clip also contains information that determines the playback speed for a certain number of frames over a specific time period. This is known as *FPS*, or *Frames Per Second*, and it is the measurement of the frame rate of a moving image.

Here is one last tidbit of information related to frame rate that can be useful. The frame rate can be used to calculate how many frames are actually in a movie by multiplying the FPS by the length of the movie (in seconds): 30FPS × 1000 sec (length of movie) = 30,000 frames. This calculation may be handy when combined with other data like frame size and color depth (e.g. 8-bit) for determining the file size and the amount of compression necessary for optimum playback performance.

53

TIPS FOR OPTIMUM PLAYBACK PERFORMANCE

All media servers are optimized to perform to the manufacturer's specification provided you do your part. When you read that a media server can play four movies at 30FPS without dropping frames, it is best not to assume that you can use just any piece of content you want and achieve those results. Manufacturers recommend specific file formats and codecs that allow the system to perform up to those claims. Preparing your content according to these specifications helps ensure the media server plays it back the way it was intended.

While there should always be an emphasis on maximizing the server's performance, the overall quality of the image cannot be sacrificed. Do some simple testing with your content on the system before the first day of programming so you can determine if there are any changes that need to be made to help the system perform correctly.

CHAPTER 8

Optimizing Content Playback from the Console

Once content has been loaded on a media server, the digital lighting programmer's work is not finished. At that point, the content's maximum performance potential can still be adjusted. Since no two devices are the same, how is the best way to do that? There is no real shortcut. The best way is to play a piece of content back on the media server, project it through the output device, and observe it. Since that is something that cannot usually be done ahead of load-in, last minute adjustments may need to be made to the content in order for it to match the client's expectations. In this chapter we take a look at some adjustments that can be made from the lighting console that can increase the quality of playback after the content has been loaded on the server.

Some of the adjustments that can be made to content include gamma, brightness or black levels, and contrast. Each of these adjustments will increase or decrease the luminance of an image. But what is luminance?

LUMINANCE

Luminance can be described as the amount of light being emitted by a display at a given angle. It is essentially a measure of how bright a display will appear from a particular viewing angle. Video display manufacturers of LED screens, plasma displays, LCD screens, and cathode ray tubes (CRTs) use a measure of luminance called a *nit* to describe the brightness of their products. A nit is one candela per square meter/10.76 square ft, and a typical computer display emits from around a hundred to several hundred nits. An LED display typically emits several thousand nits.

FIGURE 8.1
Luminance comparison (original image left, corrected image right).

In addition to luminance, there are a variety of factors that contribute to the appearance of an image as it is viewed on a display device. These include gamma, brightness, and contrast.

GAMMA

Gamma is a color management tool that is used to correct any irregularities in display devices. An irregularity may be introduced for various reasons, but the bottom line is that it can change the ratio between the luminance value of a pixel as it is input to the display device and the luminance value as it is actually displayed. Any distortions in the display device can be corrected by applying a gamma correction so that your eye perceives the correct brightness as it was intended across the range of luminosity. A word of caution: when using gamma to adjust the brightness of the image, the colors in the image are being adjusted, and the result is that the colors can look different than how they were intended to look.

FIGURE 8.2
Gamma comparison (original image left, corrected image right).

BRIGHTNESS

Brightness refers to the visual perception of luminance in an image. It differs from luminance in that it is how bright an image seems to be, not necessarily how bright it actually is. Video display devices depend on this illusion for contrast. When a television screen, for example, is off, the screen appears dark gray. But when it is on and a pixel is blacked out, it appears to be black, not gray. (FYI, this phenomenon is known as *video black*, and it occurs with LED panels and projectors as well.)

57

FIGURE 8.3
Brightness comparison (original image left, corrected image right).

Incorrect adjustment of the brightness in an image is a very common problem and it can result in poor image quality when the image is displayed. Take care to make sure this adjustment is correct. It is also important to pay close attention to the proper adjustment of the black levels on the display device so that the brightness of the image will not have to be distorted beyond reasonable values. If the brightness in an image is set too low, a large range of input signals will be "crushed" or compressed beyond usability. If the brightness is set too high then no input signal can achieve true black, which will cause the image to be based on values of gray. The overall contrast ratio will be lost, and the image will appear washed-out and dull. A good rule of thumb for brightness is to adjust the black levels so that black picture content displays as true black on your display device.

CONTRAST

The contrast ratio of an image is the ratio of light to dark in an image. It is a major determining factor in how the quality of an image is perceived. If an image has a high contrast ratio, it will appear to be sharper than a picture with a lower contrast ratio, even if the lower contrast picture has substantially more measurable resolution. Lower contrast ratios can appear gray or hazy whereas higher contrast ratios can cause the white areas of an image to become washed-out. Because every image can have varying amounts of light and dark, it is a good idea to check the contrast of each image in order to achieve the optimum display settings.

Making adjustments to contrast, gamma and brightness in real time is a truly unique function of using a lighting console to control a media server. The lighting programmer can assess each piece of content on the fly and make adjustments where necessary; those values can be recorded into a cue and played back from the console. And should the display

FIGURE 8.4
Contrast comparison (original image left, corrected image right).

device have to be swapped for a different device in a different venue, the content itself does not have to be re-rendered. Because you are using a lighting console, basic attribute palettes that have been stored for contrast, brightness, and gamma can be updated and all cues in the show referencing those palettes will automatically update.[10]

ALPHA CHANNEL

One additional visual effect that can be applied from the lighting console is the *alpha channel*. Typically, if you are creating an image that will be used as a visual mask over another image, an area within the masking image will need to be designated as transparent and that data will be saved within the image as an additional channel of information. However, because we are using a media server, we may have the option to apply an alpha type effect at any time to any piece of content if the media server has the feature. This

59

means that multiple layers of images can be stacked on top of each other, and where there is an alpha area, the layer beneath will be visible. This effect is very useful in situations where you want to put a background behind a corporate logo for instance, and it does not require any pre-rendering of the images.

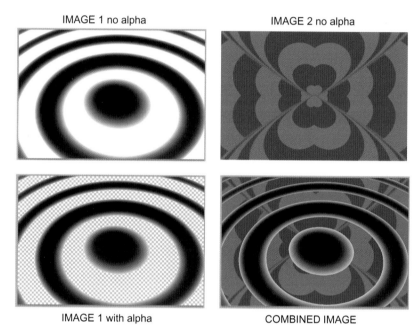

FIGURE 8.5
Images on two layers, with Alpha Channel applied.

Media servers allow images and videos to be manipulated in real time in a variety of ways. From applying color balancing to visual effects, using a media server means you have the power of a video editing software package at your fingertips without the need for any pre-rendering time. Finding creative ways to use all the channels of a server can save you from spending extra time in the video editing suite!

CHAPTER 9

Content Gone Wild: Unexpected Playback Results

It is not uncommon to encounter unexpected results during playback of content from time to time. Many factors can have an effect on the performance of the media server, both in hardware and in software. Here are a few of the more common issues that can arise, with some solutions to help you deal with an unruly piece of content or server.

ARTIFACTS

While most media servers are capable of resolutions up to 1,920 × 1,080, recent advancements in technology allow for resolutions up to 8K in some servers. The downside of using images at these high-definition (HD) resolutions is that they show a lot more detail than a standard-definition (SD) image, so the source content must be cleaner and without artifacts. What's an artifact? Basically, an artifact is anything that appears in your video when it is being played back that was not in the source material. These unwanted effects can include Blocking, Dotcrawl, Moiré, Pixelation, or Ringing. And in some cases the problem is not in the video source but an artifact of playback. If the playback mechanism fails to decode the image properly, for instance, it may drop data and could result in random color defects. The result is the same though: your content does not playback as expected, and you are left scrambling to repair the problem.[11]

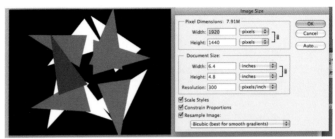

HD IMAGE

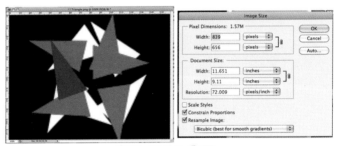

SD IMAGE

FIGURE 9.1

Comparison of clean HD image and same image in SD upscaled showing pixelation.

To repair artifacts, you will likely need to review the original source material of the content. If the content was not rendered correctly, it may require re-rendering, or even trying a different codec to achieve better results. If the source material is not of good quality though, there may not be much you can do except try to get a new image or higher resolution version of the clip you want to use.

INTERLACED VS PROGRESSIVE SCAN

Progressive scan (aka de-interlaced) video means that every pixel on the screen is refreshed in order, whereas interlaced video is displayed by drawing only a partial image first on alternating lines, then filling in the remaining lines. Whether the content you use should be interlaced is going to depend on the media server you are using. If the system is optimized for de-interlaced images, and you try to play an interlaced image on it, you are going to see many problems with the appearance, including tearing and horizontal scan lines in the image because you are going to be 'missing' some bits of data in the image in between each row, and the image quality is going to be greatly reduced.[12]

FIGURE 9.2
Image showing interlacing.

It is fairly easy to fix this problem, thankfully. The clip can be loaded into a video editing application and a de-interlace filter can be applied. Once applied, the clip is re-rendered, and when it's done, all scan lines should be history.

ASPECT RATIO

The ratio of horizontal to vertical resolution is usually 4:3, the same as that of conventional television sets, while the

16:9 widescreen format has become very popular thanks to film. However, if a 16:9 ratio clip is played back at a 4:3 ratio, it will appear distorted (in other words, stretched or squashed). Therefore, in order to maintain the correct aspect ratio in the image, it may be necessary to use *Letterbox*. Letterbox refers to the black area above and below an image that is used to fill in the "unused" areas that result from formatting the image to appear correctly on the screen.

 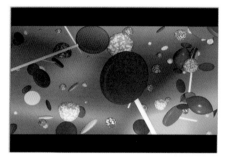

4:3   **16:9**

FIGURE 9.3
4:3 ratio, 16:9 ratio.

DROPPED FRAMES

If a clip appears to skip a frame (or several) while playing, this is known as a *dropped frame*. Nearly all unintentionally dropped frames are due either to incorrectly configured hardware or settings. A few tips that may help avoid unintentionally dropping frames are:

- Do not run multiple applications at the same time (no multitasking).
- Ensure that your hardware can handle the tasks you are asking of it. This situation occurs more regularly for programmers who install software on a media server not built by the manufacturer. If building your own server, refer to the recommended specifications for hardware.

- Configure hardware correctly. Take refresh rates, for example. A good rule of thumb to follow when choosing a refresh rate for a display device is to set it based on a multiple of the rendered FPS of the content. In other words, if the majority of the content is rendered at 30FPS, then it will be displayed correctly by selecting 30 or 60 Hz on the display device. If the bulk of content is rendered at 25FPS, on the other hand, it will be displayed correctly on a display device with a refresh rate setting of 50 or 75 Hz.[13]

SLOW LOADING SPEEDS

The trade off for using high-resolution content is slower loading speeds but compression can help offset the negative effects on the server's playback performance. Many of the Mac based media servers that prefer the Photo-JPEG codec recommend a medium quality amount of compression around 60 percent. Any compression ratio higher than 60 percent simply increases file size without any real improvement in image quality through the server.[14]

CHOPPY VIDEO PLAYBACK AT SLOWER FPS

Most automated lighting fixtures on the market today utilize 16-bit resolution for the pan and tilt channels. This resolution is visible in the fixture's movement when a lighting cue is recorded that changes the fixture's position. Other attributes such as gobo rotation may also utilize 16-bit resolution, and this will allow the rotation channel to be recorded with changes in speeds without compromising the smoothness of the rotation of the gobo. Because of these features in automated lighting, most lighting designers and programmers expect the same type of performance from a media server especially when recording cues with changes to the playspeed of a movie.

65

Many media servers feature a control channel for media playspeed. This channel can be used to slow down or speed up a piece of content. However, this may have undesirable results because when a piece of content is created, it will be rendered at a specific FPS value. When a piece of 30FPS content is being played back at its rendered speed, each frame will blend cohesively into the next. But when that same piece of content is played back at 15FPS (by overriding the content's rendered frame rate via the playspeed control channel), the content will be playing back at half of its rendered speed, and it may appear 'jerky' or 'choppy' because you have time-stretched the footage.

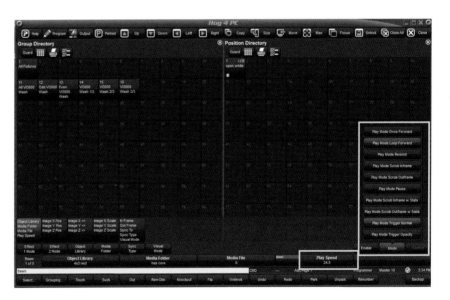

FIGURE 9.4
Hog4PC playmode toolbar.

The good news is that most media servers use a blending technique called *frame interpolation* to 'fill in the missing frames.' Frame interpolation helps create intermediate video frames based on the data in two consecutive frames of encoded video. Through a process of applying algorithms that compensate and estimate motion, intermediate pixels between frames are computed and new frames will be rendered to fill in the missing frames when played at a slower FPS speed.[15]

These are a few of the types of issues that can arise while working with a media server. When I encounter any issue during playback, I start by trying to identify the problem so that I can then find a solution. Luckily, the solution usually presents itself once I've taken some time to assess the content and the server and gone over some of the basic steps of setup again. Sometimes, it's easy, sometimes it takes a little longer; but it's always an opportunity to learn something new.

CHAPTER 10

Video Editing Applications

Specific types of content require the use of specific types of creation software. For instance, still images are generally the easiest to create, and a good place to start is to simply snap a high-resolution picture of something eye-catching with a digital camera; perhaps it can be used as a background or texture. However, if realistic pictures are not suitable for your application, perhaps you will need to create a texture completely from scratch with a graphics program; so you may need a program that works with layers, visual effects, and perhaps even text.

There are many still image/photo editing software packages available, but the primary things you will need to look for are: being able to easily adjust resolutions, image size, and saving in a variety of formats since not all media servers have the same image requirements. Adobe® Photoshop® is one of the most popular image editing applications available, and it shares common formats with Adobe After Effects so that images can be easily imported into an After Effects' composition.

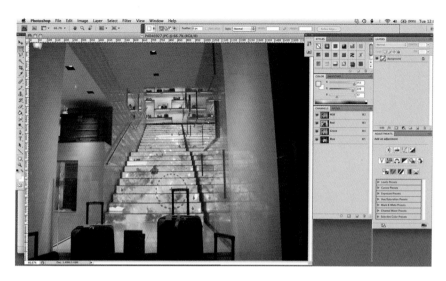

FIGURE 10.1
Adobe Photoshop.

Creating moving images, clips, and animations is a little more involved than creating still images. Important features to look for in an editing application are:

- Being able to convert from one format to another (e.g. AVI to MOV)
- Video compression tools for encoding the content with a variety of video codecs
- Timing editing tools for adjusting frame rates and playback speed
- Imaging tools for editing resolution and image size
- Ability to de-interlace video content (most digital lighting media servers recommend de-interlaced content)
- Ability to import and export captured video content easily
- Color correction capability as well as brightness and contrast ratios.

A few important things to be aware of when creating custom content:

- Particular attention should be given to the frame rate and formats of a clip before exporting for use with a media server.
- While there are many applications that can create animations, an animation (e.g. FLASH) may need to be converted to another format such as MOV or AVI before it can be used in a server.
- Effects are the unique elements that are applied to a digital animation, so software that provides a variety of graphic elements is very important. These effects can be everything from particle systems (smoke, fire, bubbles, and clouds) to banners, blurs, and distortions.

Two of the most popular applications for video editing and compositing are Adobe After Effects or Apple Final Cut Pro®.

FIGURE 10.2
After Effects.

FIGURE 10.3
Final Cut Pro.

RE-ENCODING A VIDEO CLIP

When a piece of content simply requires a different codec or format, however, the media server programmer has some less expensive options available. This process of re-encoding a clip is commonly referred to as *transcoding*, and it will require a transcoding application.

Low cost applications for performing some simple transcoding are available, and one of the most popular that can work in a pinch is QuickTime Pro.

TMPGEnc® is another transcoding application, and it is recommended by High End Systems for use with its digital lighting products that require the MPEG-2 format.

While there are plenty of shareware and low cost encoding applications available for converting to and/or from various codecs, it may be wiser and more cost effective in the

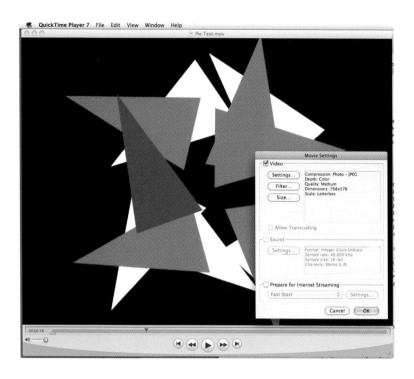

FIGURE 10.4
QuickTime Pro.

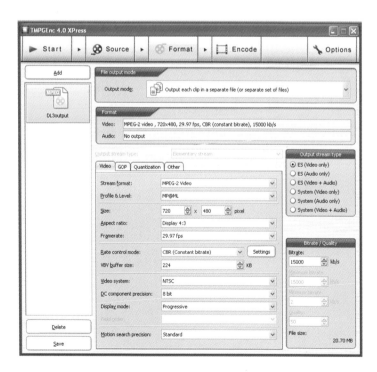

FIGURE 10.5
TMPGEnc.

long run to invest in a full featured editing suite like Adobe After Effects or Apple Final Cut Pro. And, an application like one of these is a must if you are at all interested in creating your own content. Many content creators use one or both of these. While there are other options, most will not have as many built in features and settings for compression and rendering as these, so in the end it is something to consider, especially if you are going to be working with media servers consistently.

NO ALL IN ONE SOLUTION

As you can tell, there are many different formats of digital content that can be used in media servers today. Each format is unique and has specific tools for creating and editing. While the two most popular video editing and compositing applications available are After Effects and Final Cut Pro, unfortunately there is no all in one solution when it comes to content creation software. Luckily, software developers such as Adobe and Apple offer suites and packages of applications with universal formats for easy importing and exporting between applications.[16] So do not stress about having multiple applications for content editing on your laptop; eventually your bag of editing tools will likely contain a variety of software, but that may help you when you least expect it.

CHAPTER 11

Video Copyright Laws

Digital content is domestically protected under this U.S. copyright protection:

FBI Anti-Piracy Warning

The unauthorized reproduction or distribution of this copy-righted work is illegal. Copyright infringement, including in-fringement without monetary gain, is investigated by the FBI and is punishable by up to 5 years in federal prison and a fine of $250,000.

FIGURE 11.1
FBI Copyright Logo.

I would be negligent if I wrote a book about media servers and content and did not include this extremely important topic. For anyone who works with any type of digital content, knowing how the law protects the rights of the content creators is extremely important.

A copyright is the protection of a person's creation, whether it is in digital arts, literature, music, or other media. Only the creator/owner of the media has the rights to use the material. The copyright protection is immediate; as soon as the media is created, it is protected. Proving that you created it first is the tricky part. The copyright on the media can be further established by registering it with the U.S. Copyright Office. However, an easier way to show proof of ownership is to burn a copy of it, sign it and date it, and mail it to yourself. Then when it arrives, do not open it; just tuck it away in a safe place. This is commonly known as the "poor man's copyright," and it helps establish a legal date of possession should any issue arise about ownership.

Copyrights may not seem all that important to some, but they are. While the intent may not be to keep another artist from their rightful earnings for work they have performed, the result of using another person's content that you have not rightfully paid for is doing just that. However, this is so often overlooked simply from a convenience standpoint, if for no other reason. My rule of thumb is, if it is not stock content that came with the server, and I did not buy it or make it, or the client did not supply it, then I do not use it. When I come across custom content left behind on the media server, I disregard it and I definitely do not use it. I will also notify the company that rented the server that they should remove all non-stock content from the server before renting it again. No one wants to have their hard work 'borrowed' and used without rightful credit and/or payment, so

I strongly urge everyone who programs with media servers to never use any media content that they do not have the rights to use. And for this reason, I always remove all custom content that I have added to a server at the end of the show, before I shut down the server. I strongly encourage you to never leave content that you have added on the media server if it is going back to a rental house or has a chance of being used on another show; if it gets used, and the rightful owner sees it, you could be in big trouble.

So remember:

- Use only stock content that is preloaded on the server or content that you have the rights to use (purchased or created). This includes knowing if the client has the legal rights to use a piece of content that they hand you.
- Do not leave custom content on a server once a show ends.
- Do not use content from another show left behind on a server.

This common sense approach to content usage is safe and will help ensure the rights of all parties.

INTERNATIONAL COPYRIGHT

U.S. copyright protection is only binding on U.S. soil. The bad news is that there is unfortunately no easy way to protect your content once it finds its way into another country. The content becomes subject to that country's specific laws, and it may also be furthered protected under an international treaty known as the Berne Convention for the Protection of Literary and Artistic Works, although there is no guarantee. So, the best way to protect yourself is to make sure not to leave any of your personal content behind once the show ends.

CHAPTER 12

Preparing for a Show

How do you prepare for a gig with a media server? When you accept the job, there are a few questions that should be asked in order to make your job a lot easier onsite. In this chapter we will examine a few of the essential steps you can take to be prepared before arriving on the job site.

In addition to the media server(s), you may need other pieces of gear to make the connections between console, server, and display devices. I highly recommend taking the time to draw out the control signal path as well as the video signal path ahead of time to make sure you know how many and what kinds of cables or any special adapters may be needed to connect everything together. It can also help you make sense of the spaghetti seen in Figure 12.1.

Many people use Nemetschek Vectorworks® or another type of CAD drawing application for this purpose, and I regularly use a flowchart application called OmniGraffle®. Basically any type of drawing application may also work. In this age of networking and computers, it is very helpful to think through the full setup on paper before load-in day. Planning out the layout helps avoid many surprises onsite and ensures that setup will happen smoothly.

FIGURE 12.1
FOH cables.

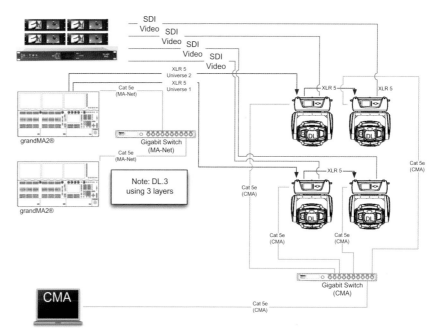

FIGURE 12.2
FOH wiring diagram
drawn in OmniGraffle.

Below is a pre-show checklist with some suggestions on steps you can take to be prepared for the gig.

PREP STEP #1. DETERMINE THE GEAR YOU NEED FOR THE PROJECT

Here is a checklist with a minimum set of questions related to the setup and operation of the equipment that will help get you started:

1. Media Server
   - ✓ Is your media server controlled via DMX or another type of protocol (e.g. Art-Net, MIDI, or operated stand-alone)?
   - ✓ What kind of hardware is involved in connecting the media server to the console?
   - ✓ What kind of video signal does the media server output?
   - ✓ How many video outputs does the server have?
   - ✓ Which outputs are assigned to which display devices?
   - ✓ How will that signal be distributed to the display device(s)?
   - ✓ What is the display resolution?
   - ✓ What is the refresh rate for the display device(s)?
2. Lighting Control Console
   - ✓ What lighting console will you be using?
   - ✓ How many channels does your media server need for control, and does your lighting console have enough available channels and DMX universes?
   - ✓ Is the software version in the lighting console current?
   - ✓ Does the software in the lighting console include the latest fixture profile for the type of media server you are using? *Note*: Digital lighting is a bleeding

edge technology, and software versions change rapidly. As such, it is not unusual for a lighting console to include a library that is out of date or inaccurate. Knowing what version of the fixture personality is included in a console's library is crucial to being able to use all available features of any lighting equipment.

3. **Display Devices**
- ✓ What types of devices are being used?
- ✓ If using projectors, what is the image projection surface?
- ✓ If using LEDs, what is the pixel pitch needed for best viewing?
- ✓ What size will the image be?
- ✓ Are there available hanging positions for the optimum distance between projectors and screens?
- ✓ What video signal cable and connectors are suitable options for the equipment you are using?
- ✓ Which signal choice is best suited for your application?

Being prepared may also lead you to ask, "Should I carry extra hardware like cables, adapters, or hard drives?" My opinion is that if there is any doubt as to whether or not the right equipment will be available onsite, the answer is yes. It is better to be prepared than to be without the correct adapter that you need to connect device A to device B. But how far do you go with that idea? Extra connectors and a spare cable can easily fit into a gig bag, so those are essentials. Extra hard drives or video equipment like scan converters are more helpful in applications where the show is in a remote area and backups are not readily available. Any equipment that is larger than something you can carry can usually be negotiated ahead of time and supplied by the local company providing the gear.

PREP STEP #2. OPTIMIZING YOUR MEDIA SERVER HARDWARE FOR BETTER PERFORMANCE

Display Resolution

It is important to optimize the settings for the video outputs of the server *before* launching the media server application to ensure the best performance of the video content. After powering up the server, open up the Display Settings (System Preferences on a Mac or Control Panel on a PC) before you launch the media server application and set your display resolution to the settings recommended for the media server and for the type of display device being used.

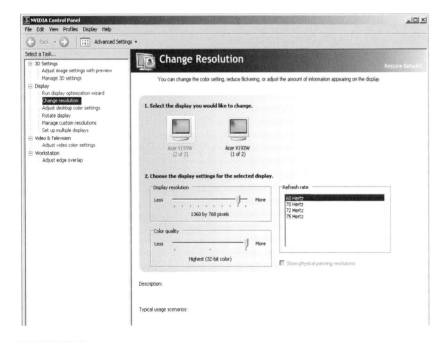

FIGURE 12.3
PC control panel showing screen resolution info.

Display Refresh Rates

The second setting that should be checked and reset if necessary is the refresh rate for the display device. The adjustment for refresh rate is also found in the Display Settings window. It is good practice to select a refresh rate that the display device can handle but nothing higher than what is recommended (it could actually do harm, although more than likely, you will just not see anything on that device or you may see "Out of Range").

What does the term *refresh rate* refer to? The refresh rate is the frequency at which a monitor can update its display; this value is expressed in Hertz (Hz). Note that one potential problem area for computers is that refresh rates differ between different graphics cards and monitors so it is best to test your content on your server and check the refresh rate if your video clip appears to be running at the wrong speed. The one refresh rate that all LCD monitors can handle is 60 Hz, so if in doubt, start there.

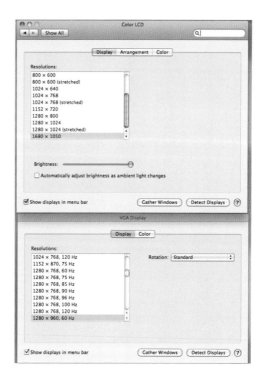

FIGURE 12.4
MAC OS control panel showing refresh rate info.

FIGURE 12.5
Catalyst and ArKaos FPS statistics.

Many media servers (Catalyst and ArKaos are shown in Figure 12.5) provide onscreen performance feedback windows for FPS, GPU, and other statistics to better help you troubleshoot issues like dropped frames, sluggish playback, and other playback related irregularities.

PREP STEP #3. LOADING CONTENT ON A SERVER

An important aspect of digital lighting that should not be overlooked is the process of uploading, organizing, and managing your digital video content when working with media servers. For many practical reasons, it is worth the time to set up the server and load all content prior to the first day of programming, if at all possible. If you have not yet tried copying custom content into a media server, then you are going to be in for a shock. Transferring large quantities of digital content from external drives to a media server can bring everything to a screeching halt and prevent you from being able to do anything else until all of your servers complete the loading process. And most media servers require you to physically be in front of the server while loading content, renaming your files for better organization, and configuring the server, so it makes sense to try to do all these things ahead of time if you can.

A huge plus for loading content before load-in day is that it gives you a chance to power up the server and make sure it is in acceptable working condition and loaded with the correct software version. Once the content has been loaded into the server and everything checks out as functioning, you can check the playback performance of your content by either connecting the lighting console and triggering the content or manually executing the content from the media server's user interface (if available). If there are any issues with playback performance, those issues can be more easily dealt with at that time than when you arrive onsite at the gig and are without the software and hardware you need to make any necessary changes to the content.[17]

An additional note about content organization; content should be organized ahead of time. Placing content into folders named for each song is one example of how content can be organized. On DMX controllable servers, media files have to be organized in such a way that they can be accessed via a DMX lighting console.

One example of content organization is demonstrated in Figure 12.6 with the Mbox® Studio software. The DMX protocol for all Mbox products contains a DMX control channel for media folders and a DMX control channel for media files. These two channels work together; in other words, they are dependent on each other for the selection of a media file. The way it works is simple: the programmer selects a folder via the corresponding DMX channel on the console and then

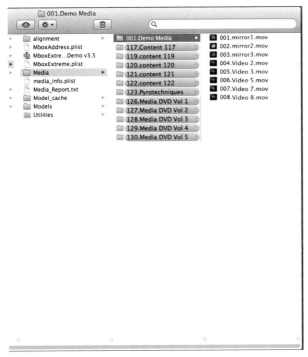

FIGURE 12.6
Screen capture showing file numbering schemes in Mbox.

selects a file within that folder via its corresponding DMX channel. In order for the files to be correctly selected though, the individual files have to be organized into separate folders and then individually numbered using a 3-digit value between 000 and 255. Again, using the Mbox as an example, this labeling scheme for folders follows the format "001. mymediafolder." Inside each of the individual folders will be the individual media files also numbered according to the same scheme "001.mymediafile.mov." With the potential number of content reaching over 65,000 files (256 files multiplied by 256 folders), hopefully you can see why organization is a critical part of programming with a media server.

The example in Figure 12.6 is only one way content can be organized on a server. Some servers such as the Hippotizer allow the user to simply drag and drop content directly into the application, no pre-numbering (or pre-encoding) required.

FIGURE 12.7
Hippotizer MediaManager.

It is also important for the content to be organized and documented if the show has the potential to be remounted in the future. This is a very common occurrence on cruise ships, for instance. A show will typically be created on one ship and then distributed throughout the entire cruise line fleet. So organization is a must. And in the organization process, it is a great idea to include thumbnails of the content as well, so that you can be assured you have all of the content needed for the show. These thumbnails also make it a lot easier to locate a piece of content, especially when time has passed between shows. Thumbnails are usually stored locally on media servers and can be copied; but in the worst case scenario, a simple screen capture can work as well.

As every server has its own unique approach, it is definitely a good idea to familiarize yourself with the best organizational approach that matches the server you will be using. And though all of these preparations may seem like common sense, they will help alleviate stress onsite and will help give you more time to focus on programming.

CHAPTER 13

Networking Servers

The use of networks in entertainment applications has opened up the door to a range of new possibilities in terms of working with multiple computers at one time. This is especially true with regards to controlling media servers. Since all media servers are computer based applications, the server's built-in networking capabilities can be utilized, making setup and control a bit simpler. In this chapter we will focus on Ethernet based control and supporting applications designed to work with media servers via a network.

NETWORK BASICS

In order to use any type of network based communication between computers, each server on a network must be assigned a unique device ID; this ID number is referred to as the IP address and uses this format:

xxx.xxx.xxx.xxx   e.g. 192.168.1.101

While lighting programmers may not be as familiar with networking, the concept of using an IP address can be compared directly to the way lighting programmers assign a unique number to a fixture (called its *DMX address*) in order to patch the fixture in the console. Every fixture on a universe has to have a unique DMX address in order for it to be controlled independently of other fixtures on the same link. This is also true when networking computers together. You can think of the IP address of each network device as being like the DMX address of a lighting fixture: you will want a unique IP address for every device on the network.

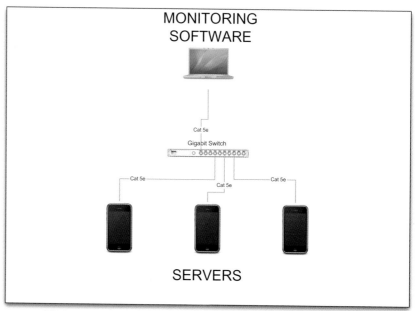

MONITORING
SOFTWARE

Cat 5e

Gigabit Switch

Cat 5e

Cat 5e

Cat 5e

SERVERS

SIMPLE NETWORK FOR REMOTE MONITORING

FIGURE 13.1
Networking diagram for monitoring multiple servers.

Note: It is necessary to use an Ethernet switch when connecting multiple network devices, and every fixture must have a direct line to the switch because Ethernet cannot be daisy chained together like DMX. This configuration is referred to as a *star* network.

ART-NET

In recent years the lighting industry has embraced the use of transmitting control signals over Ethernet. One type of control signal commonly implemented in most lighting consoles is Art-Net by Artistic License. Art-Net allows a DMX signal to be sent over a Cat5/5e/6 cable to Art-Net compliant devices on the same network, thus eliminating the need for 5-pin XLR DMX cables.

When the console and media server are connected via Art-Net, then the IP addresses of both the console and the server will need to be within the same range. Art-Net IPs typically use an address in either the 2.x.x.x or 10.x.x.x range. If your server has an IP of 2.0.0.1, for instance, then the console will need an IP address of 2.0.0.x (where x represents any number between 2 and 255).

In addition to an IP address, the computer network that all of the devices are connected to will be assigned a *subnet mask* number. This number also uses the x.x.x.x format and is usually something like 255.x.x.x (255.255.255.0, for instance). As long as all of the devices connected to a single network are assigned the same subnet mask and each has an individual IP address, then all devices will communicate nicely with each other.

MEDIA SERVER SUPPORT APPLICATIONS

Some other important server management tasks are also now much simpler due to the convenience of having a network that connects computers together. Below are some of the applications available for remotely accessing and controlling a media server via a network.

Content Management

When it comes to loading content onto servers, there is no one size fits all solution. The truth is, you have quite a few options available primarily because of networking capabilities. For instance, whether you are using a Mac or PC, you

93

can create a shared folder on the server and then by simply connecting to other computers on the network as a guest, all computers can transfer files between each other by copying files into the shared folder. That is a solution that will work in a pinch, but it isn't the only option available to users of some media servers. Several server developers have created support applications that work in conjunction with the primary media server application and enable the user to perform a variety of additional functions (e.g. loading content, assigning DMX values, configuring modes) from a remote computer. One such application is the CMA.

After High End Systems launched the Axon media server in 2006, following the release of the DL.2®, the company released a free supporting software application called the Content Management Application, or, as it is more commonly referred to, the CMA. The CMA features digital-to-digital file transfer capabilities, which can greatly increase the efficiency of uploading content to a server via network based delivery. The CMA can be very helpful to the digital lighting programmer. For instance, content can be uploaded and transferred between servers simply using drag and drop type functionality anytime without having to be in front of the media server(s), and having to restart the media server(s) after loading new content. This enables the programmer to spend less time on content management and more time on the creative process once onsite. The CMA also allows the user to remotely upgrade the media server's software, and it provides the ability to remotely assign DMX values to a server's content files once they have been loaded. Once content has been uploaded to the server(s), the content can be previewed at the remote location via thumbnails that are created for each piece of content. These thumbnails are displayed in the CMA window, along with the DMX number and name of the file, so content is easily recognizable and accessible. This greatly reduces the need for paper copies of thumbnails of each file to be kept on hand as well as streamlining the searching and sorting processes while programming.[18]

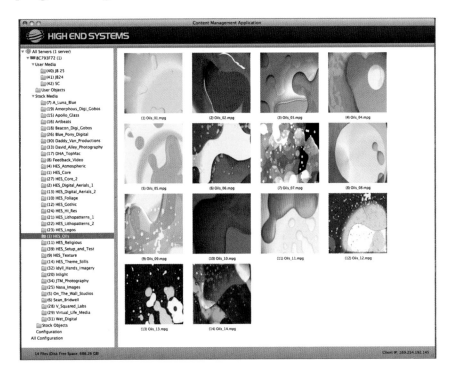

FIGURE 13.2
Screen capture from CMA.

Remote Monitoring

Some media servers allow for remote monitoring of all media servers on the same network. Remote monitoring can be very helpful for monitoring status and performance while also providing an access point into the server from a remote location. PRG and Green Hippo both have created support applications for their media servers which are useful tools while programming.

One example of a remote monitoring application is Mbox® Remote. Mbox Remote allows the user to monitor the status of FPS, timecode, effects, and layer activity to name but a few functions. This application also features a media window that shows a thumbnail for each piece of content contained in the media directory folders. I particularly like this application for its flexibility in that it allows me remote access to the actual desktop of the Mbox I am interacting with, and it gives me physical controls for the server such as shutdown and relaunch from a remote location, for instance. This means that if the servers are locked away in a room somewhere I cannot get to, I still have access to the servers remotely.

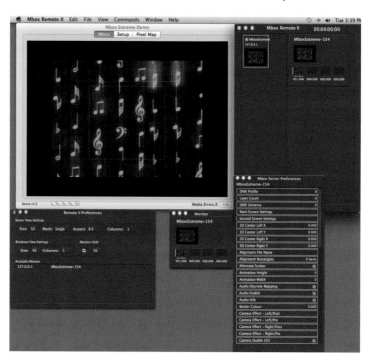

FIGURE 13.3
Screen capture from Mbox Remote.

In 2008 Green Hippo also released ZooKeeper™, its own remote server management application. The ZooKeeper application allows you to remotely monitor and control the layers and attributes of all Hippotizers on a HippoNet network from a remote Graphical User Interface (GUI).

ZooKeeper also allows the user control of all major functions of the Hippotizer, including:

- Importing and encoding content
- Accessing all controls for every layer of every connected Hippotizer
- Configuring display settings
- Saving presets
- Creating timelines
- Enabling and disabling components
- Creating and assigning pixel maps.

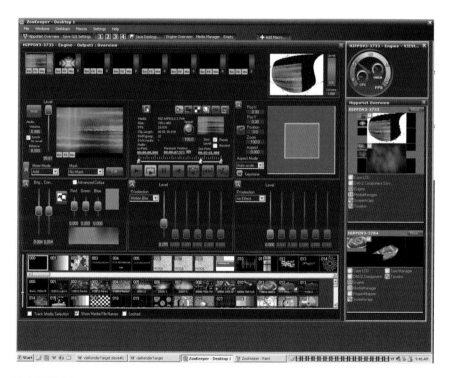

FIGURE 13.4
Green Hippo Hippotizer and ZooKeeper.

Built in Network Monitoring

Some media servers have incorporated remote monitoring directly into the graphical user interface. One example of

97

this is from within Catalyst. Catalyst features several HUDs (Heads Up Displays) that not only report the internal status of the server, but also allow the programmer to remotely monitor any other server on the same network. This eliminates the need for any additional software to be running on the same network and puts the controls for the information directly at the fingertips of the programmer via the keyboard hotkeys mapped into Catalyst's interface.

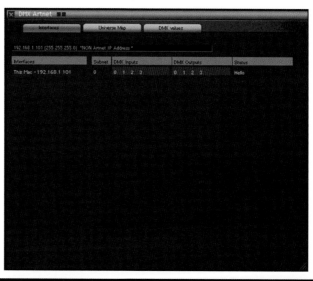

FIGURE 13.5
Catalyst network monitoring HUD.

As networking continues to evolve, the practicality for using it in entertainment settings also increases. Whether it's loading new content or simply changing the DMX address of a server remotely, the flexibility of remote monitoring far outweighs the cost in both time and energy spent in doing some of the mundane tasks of working with a media server. Most are free, if not already included in the GUI of the server, so take the time to download them all and then you will have them when you need them on site.

CHAPTER 14

Streaming Video

As the popularity of media servers has grown, so has the need for better feedback at FOH and on the lighting console. In situations where the media servers are not located next to the lighting console, the lighting programmer can be at a real disadvantage. With only DMX cables connecting FOH to a media server backstage somewhere, the status of the media server at any given time can be a big question mark for the programmer. That is, unless the media server has a way of communicating with a remote location and sending status information and possibly even streaming video images. In an effort to accommodate this need to see what's happening with the server at any given time, media server software engineers have developed some new protocols for streaming live video images and/or thumbnails between the server and a lighting console or remote monitoring computer via Ethernet.

CITP PROTOCOL

Capture Visualisation AB, a fast growing and innovative visualization software company, developed an open network protocol called CITP/MSEX in the mid-2000s. Companies such as ChamSys and ArKaos quickly embraced this new communication platform and incorporated it into their software. As the software continued to be developed, companies such as Martin, ETC® and Green Hippo have followed suit by implementing this protocol into products like Maxedia, ETC® Congo®, and Hippotizer.

FIGURE 14.1
CITP thumbnails snapshot from Mbox® Director.

The importance of the CITP protocol is that it allows for the sharing of video and/or thumbnails in real time between a media server and a lighting console, remote monitoring application, or a visualizer. CITP works by transmitting a layer of data for live streaming video from the media server (MSEX) over Art-Net (Ethernet), and this stream also includes layers for DMX, information for selections of fixtures, reports, and patching (PINF, SDMX, FPTC, FSEL, FINF, and OMEX).

WHAT IS CITP?

CITP standards posted on the workgroup website www.citp-protocol.org explain:

> CITP is an open protocol for integration of lighting controllers, media servers and visualizers on a higher-than-control level. It makes it possible to browse a media server with thumbnail previews of content as well as effects, to use the correct effect-specific parameter names while programming and to preview output from a controller or visualizer. It also allows bidirectional DMX, device selection and patch transfer to and from visualizers.

MSEX: MEDIA SERVER EXTENSIONS LAYER

The Media Server Extensions layer is used for communication with media servers and allows information for specified elements to be passed from the media server to the console and/or visualizer. There are currently eight element categories included in the data stream:

1. Media (images and video)
2. Effects
3. Cues
4. Crossfades
5. Masks
6. Blend presets
7. Effect presets
8. Image presets.

MSEX 1.0 is based on the adopted media server standard of using one DMX channel to control the media library and one to control the media file. In this configuration, MSEX

1.0 can transmit information for up to 256 libraries, with each containing up to 256 items (clips). Even though currently most media servers are not designed around 3 DMX channels to control library and file elements, MSEX 1.1 expands the data that can be transmitted between devices to three library levels with a maximum of 256 discrete elements each and has been implemented in several lighting consoles, media servers, and visualization applications.

Consoles with CITP enabled features:

- grandMA2®
- ChamSys® MagicQ™
- Martin M1™
- PRG V676®
- Jands® Vista™.

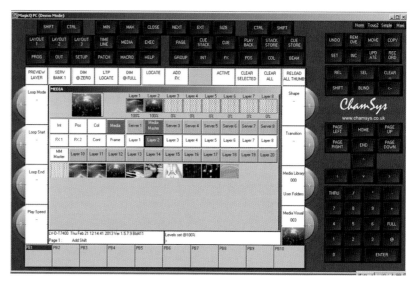

FIGURE 14.2
CITP desktop snapshot from ChamSys MagicQ.

Media servers with CITP enabled features:

- ArKaos MediaMaster Pro
- PRG Mbox® Designer

- Green Hippo Hippotizer
- Coolux® Pandoras Box.

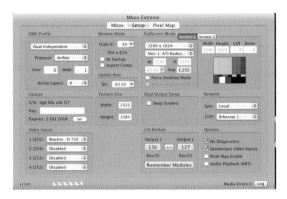

FIGURE 14.3
CITP preferences in Mbox.

Visualizers with CITP enabled features[19]:

- Capture™ Polar
- Light Converse™
- WYSIWYG®.

FIGURE 14.4
CITP preferences in WYSIWYG.

PROPRIETARY VIDEO CONTROL

The manufacturers of two media servers, the grandMA® Video Processing Unit (MA™ VPU) and the Ai® Infinity, have also released consoles that use proprietary communication to allow video images from the server to appear directly on the console. Once the grandMA2 and the MA VPU are connected in a session, thumbnails from the server will appear in the preset buttons on the console. And the Sapphire™ Media Controller is the proprietary lighting and media console that is capable of controlling the Ai Infinity server with full access to all features of the server directly on the console, including video playback. Both of these implementations are designed to offer the programmer a streamlined programming experience using proprietary languages.

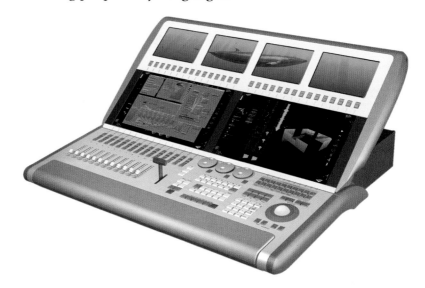

FIGURE 14.5
Sapphire Media Controller.

ADVANTAGES OF STREAMING VIDEO INTEGRATION IN LIGHTING CONSOLES

The situation I described at the beginning of this chapter is exactly why lighting consoles that can display streaming video and other data from a media server have big advantages over consoles that only display DMX values for a media server's channels. If a lighting programmer has no feedback at FOH as to the status of a server, then the only way anyone can tell that the server is working as expected is at the moment the programmer presses the **GO** button on a lighting cue—the same moment the audience gets to see the images on the screens. Talk about anxiety!

SYPHON

In situations where you don't intend to use Art-Net, but you still want to be able to view live streaming video from the media server to another application, you may have the option of using Syphon™. On the developer's website http://syphon.v002.info, Syphon is described as:

> Syphon is an open source Mac OS X technology that allows applications to share frames—full frame rate video or stills—with one another in real-time.

More commonly found in the quickly evolving market of live performance/VJ/DJ software, Syphon opens up the possibility for a media server to be used with a rapidly growing number of third party software applications that act as plug-ins to each other in a way. Some of the applications currently implementing Syphon functionality include:

- MADMapper™
- ArKaos MediaMaster Pro
- Quartz® Composer
- Modul8™
- Resolume™ 4 Arena
- Max/MSP™
- QLab™ 3.

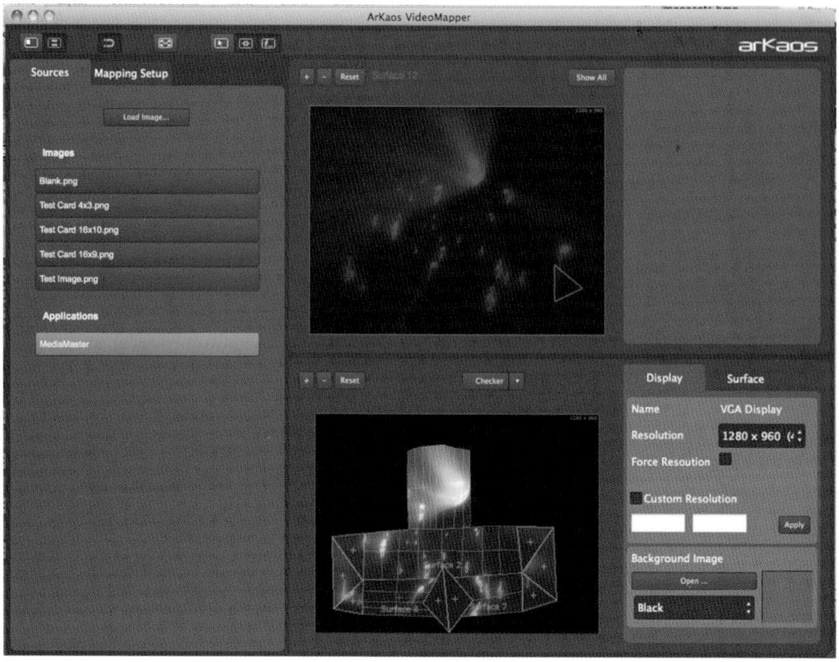

FIGURE 14.6
Syphon in ArKaos Video Mapper.

HMAP2

Green Hippo also recognized the need for a media server and a lighting console to be able to communicate in pictures instead of numbers so they created a specific component called HMap2 Server that allows the transmission of video over a HippoNet network between the Hippotizer and visualization programs such as Light Converse or ESP Vision®. This means that streaming video and thumbnails can appear on the console just like bitmaps of gobos. The HMap2 Server component is also a practical alternative to CITP over ArtNet when controlling the Hippo with consoles such as the MA Lighting grandMA2, ChamSys MagicQ, Avolite® Pearl® Expert, or other consoles that utilize HippoNet connectivity. And visualizers such as ESP Vision have also implemented HMap2 connectivity for use with the Hippotizer.

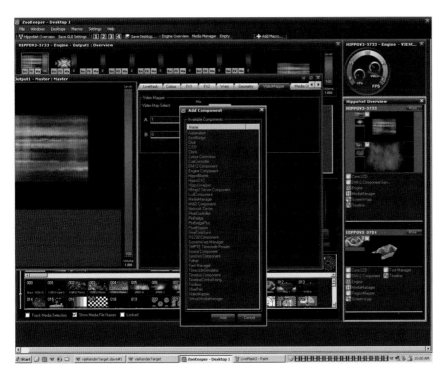

FIGURE 14.7
HMap2 component in Hippotizer.

The evolution of new technology is an endless journey and new options for versatile control solutions are continually launched at tradeshows worldwide. As the market's demand for hybrid lighting/video controllers grows, so will the level of sophistication in the type of consoles being developed… as well as the level of knowledge the programmer will need to have to use them!

CHAPTER 15

Managing Content across Multiple Outputs

In the majority of productions that contain projection, the desired size of the projected image will determine how many and what types of projectors will be necessary to cover the area. While traditional video engineers and projectionists have been managing the organization and blending of multiple projectors into one image for years, lighting programmers are beginning to take on this task because of the evolution of features in many media servers today. In this chapter we will take a look at some of the software and hardware options in DMX controlled media servers that allow a single image to be blended across multiple display devices.

PROJECTORS

The first step to any type of project using projection is choosing (or at least gathering information on) the type and number of projectors needed to cover the projection area. When using multiple projectors, attention and care must be given to the positioning of all projectors in order to be as accurate as possible. Details like hanging height, angle, and distance between the projector's lens and the screen are extremely important because this will minimize the amount of distortion in the projected image.

Lens size is also critical to make sure the image utilizes the maximum number of available pixels in the image.[20] Lens choices are numerous for professional projectors, so choosing the correct lens is very important and will be based on two factors: screen width and throw distance. In order to determine the correct lens for the application, you will need to know its *throw ratio*. To determine this, start by measuring the distance from the front of the projector to the screen (throw distance). Once you have that information, the next piece of information needed is the screen size (or projection area size). When you have these two pieces of data, divide the throw distance by the screen size. This will give you the approximate throw ratio. The formula looks like this:

$$(\text{Projector throw ratio}) \times (\text{screen width})$$
$$= \text{throw distance (distance from lens to screen)}$$

Example: If throw distance is 18 ft and the screen width is 12 feet, then you would need a lens with a ratio of 1.5.

One last note: Since projectors have zoom lenses, the resulting ratio will typically be included within a range for the lens, e.g. 1.5:1

FIGURE 15.1
Barco®HD projector.

COLLAGE GENERATOR (AXON/DL.3)

The Collage Generator® (High End Systems) allows the lighting programmer the ability to configure any number of projectors and/or DL.3 units into a single display area using DMX channels. With the selection of a DMX value on the Global Effects channel, the programmer is able to use two additional modifier channels to determine the number of X and Y panels in a grid that represents the entire collage. So, if your goal is to create a collage using six projectors with six Axons or six DL.3s, you could create a grid of either three servers wide by two projectors tall, or two wide by three tall. Once you have assigned each Axon or DL.3 a unique channel value that corresponds to its location in this grid, a single image from one of the servers will be processed into segments and distributed across all of the servers in the correct configuration. In other words, when projecting the image, each one of the servers in the collage will only be projecting its particular piece of the clip instead of the entire image. With proper alignment of each server/DL.3, the image will appear as whole.

113

Where the edges of each section of the collage overlap, some blending of the images will be necessary. DL.3 and Axon both contain edge-blending controls which apply an algorithm to the pixels in the areas of overlap to create a seamless blend by reducing the color and brightness of those areas until the overlap is not visible to the eye. Projectionists can spend hours perfecting the blend. The advantage when using a media server is that it is controlled from a lighting console instead of a small hand held remote, and it can be adjusted more easily should there be a need to switch out a projector.

FIGURE 15.2
DL.3 3 × 3 collage.

114

VIDEOMAPPER (HIPPOTIZER)

VideoMapper (Green Hippo) allows you to map a single output from the Hippotizer to multiple projection devices in much the same way that an LED processor works with LED tiles. When using the VideoMapper component, you are able to store custom mappings of any number of devices (referred to as *tiles*). When the tiles are added to the map, you are able to enter the correct pixel width of each tile, and tiles can be arranged into rows and columns of practically any configuration inside an image area up to 4,096 pixels wide x 4,096 pixels high. Once a map has been saved, it can be applied to the output of the Hippotizer easily and quickly via the VideoMapper tab in the master output layer.

Important note: when creating a map that will include several display devices, the map's resolution will need to be large enough to cover all devices and should also include negative space in between each device (if any).

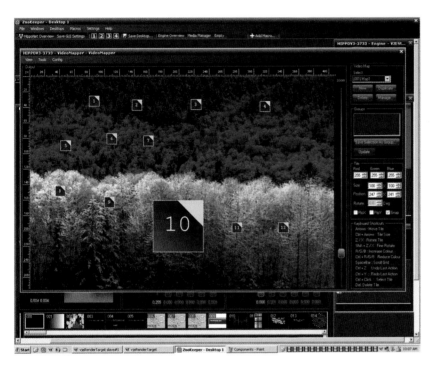

FIGURE 15.3
Hippotizer VideoMapper.

UBERPAN (HIPPOTIZER)

Similar to VideoMapper, UberPan™ is a component that allows multiple Hippotizers to work together on a HippoNet network to create a single display area of practically any resolution. Once configured, all of the Hippotizers on the network are seen as one single server, and the UberPan component handles the distribution of media across all servers.

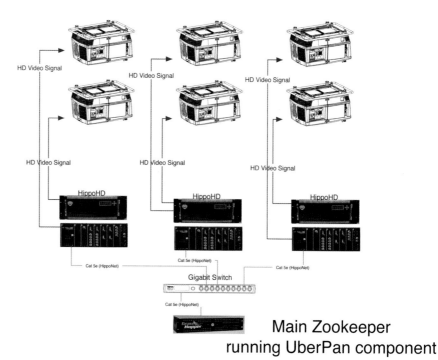

FIGURE 15.4
UberPan diagram.

ARKAOS VIDEO MAPPER (MEDIAMASTER PRO)

The Video Mapper extension allows rectangle and/or triangle surfaces (shapes that are very much like the mesh vertices used in 3D models) to be added and arranged into virtually endless configurations, and then each individual layer can be assigned a completely independent output map. When you need a single layer mapped to all surfaces, the Video Mapper extension handles that too, and it allows you to create surface maps with cropped areas that reference specific areas within a single output.

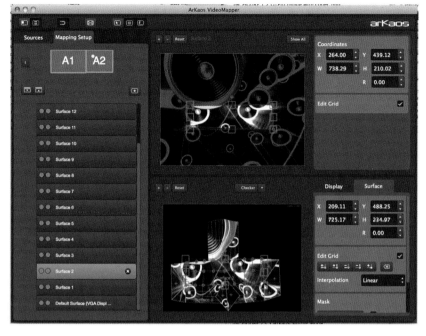

FIGURE 15.5
ArKaos Video Mapper.

117

INTERNAL BLENDING (AI)

The Ai Infinity (Avolites Media) is a new generation of media server. Its internal 3D visualizer allows you to create any type of device configuration you can dream up via the use of its Salvation™ Engine, a node based system that is user configurable. You begin creating the blend in the Stage Construction page by inserting a screen, and then you can insert any number of projectors (fixtures) and adjust their alignment on the screen. Using the Salvation Engine to patch, you connect the projectors' output to the screen and you end up with a virtual representation of what the blend will be when you arrive onsite. The advantage of using a 3D visualization server like the Ai is that when you arrive and the projectors are not in the ideal hanging locations, you can easily adjust their settings in the Ai to correct the problem without having to re-render any content or re-program any lighting cues.

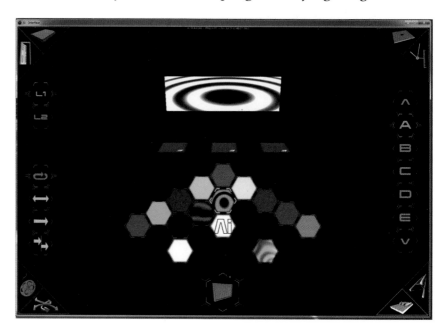

FIGURE 15.6
3 projector blend using Ai.

INTERNAL BLENDING (D3)

The d3® (d3 Technologies) is a complete integrated system of show visualization and playback. Based on a 3D simulator of the stage that can be manipulated in real time, you start by adding a 3D model of the projection surface and then add the number of projectors you need. The virtual projectors can be adjusted directly in the server, and then when you arrive onsite, you can make any necessary adjustments to positioning to correct for any issues in placement or obstructions. The d3 will take care of recalculating all the angles for the projection of the media across multiple projectors, making this type of media server especially handy for large-scale outdoor shows and architectural applications.

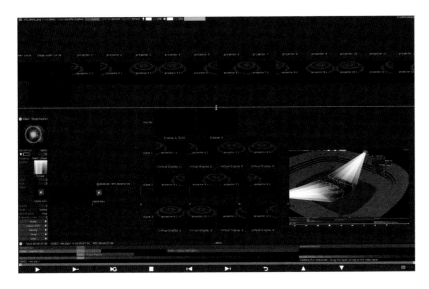

FIGURE 15.7
12 projector blend using d3.

EDGE BLEND (PANDORAS BOX)

Pandoras Box (Coolux) allows for multiple projectors (referred to as *cameras*) to be added to a Sequence timeline, and then using X offsets for each camera, a blend of multiple devices can easily be created. Layers of content can then be dragged and dropped onto the cameras and then scaled and sized to fit across all cameras.

119

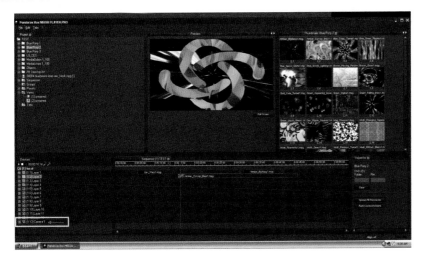

FIGURE 15.8
Pandoras Box: camera in timeline.

PANORAMIC WIDE/DUAL (MBOX DESIGNER AND STUDIO)

The dual outputs of all variations of the Mbox software (PRG) can be configured so that both outputs can be combined into one wide panoramic image. In Panoramic Dual mode, you have independent controls for keystone correction and shutter for each output; in Panoramic Wide mode, you have one master set of keystone and shutter controls for both outputs.

FIGURE 15.9
Mbox Studio panoramic wide.

While many options exist for displaying an image across multiple display devices, it is best to consider the amount of extra workload this may put on the lighting programmer especially if the programmer is also working with the lighting. In order to make sure the project runs as smoothly as possible, it may be best to add a second programmer to the gig who can focus on one of these tasks specifically. Or in some cases, using a DMX controlled media server for blending may not be the option that the video director prefers to use, and they may bring in a separate video blend system with an operator. There is nothing wrong with any of these options; it all depends on budget, time, and preference. But it does pay to know all of your options because one day it may come in handy.

CHAPTER 16

Creative Raster Planning

So what happens when you are using a media server that only has a maximum of two outputs, but you have three or more LED screens to fill up with content? Well, if the budget does not allow for adding more equipment, then the answer lies in a little bit of creative pixel planning.

THE RASTER

Every display has a finite number of pixels that are usable; this display area is known as the *raster*. Since the raster has a specific number of pixels that are determined by the resolution of the display, this area of pixels can easily be subdivided into as many areas as necessary, with each area representing one of the video displays that you have to fill with content. Once the areas are defined and carefully plotted out, video clips can be positioned into each area using the X and Y positioning controls for each layer and then sized according to the available pixels in that specific area.

For example, let's say you have one output of 1280×1024 resolution and it will be routed through an LED processor and distributed to two separate sections of LED wall. In order to get two unique images out of one video output you will need to start by determining what the maximum resolution is for each section of LED wall. In this example, I will divide the resolution in half, so that I end up with two halves equivalent to 640 × 1024 resolution. Then I select a layer, bring up intensity, and adjust its position on the screen using the layer's X and Y controls until I get the layer positioned onto one of the sections of LED wall. I will likely have to also adjust both scale of the layer and aspect ratio in order to get the size right as well (some stretching may occur as the image will be taller than it is wide). Once I have done that for the first layer, I then select a second layer and do the same thing but on the other section of LED wall. And with a little additional sizing, each half of the wall will eventually display a separate layer. Essentially, this is the basic idea behind creative pixel planning.

WORKING WITH HD CONTENT

A popular HD content format is 1080p; this refers to 1920 × 1080 progressive (non-interlaced) resolution. 1080p rendered content requires more processing power, so running several layers of HD content simultaneously can put a strain on a media server. In order to eliminate any problems with content playback, most servers have a recommended limit on the number of layers possible for playing HD content simultaneously. However, a work around for this is to size your content accurately enough so that when a single video signal is output to the display system, sections of the overall image are displayed on each screen instead of the entire image on every screen. The key to using this method of image display is to render a single piece of content that incorporates all of the individual pieces of HD content. Then, the server only has to play one video on one layer instead of many. And since multiple clips are rendered into one image, it actually appears that there are multiple images on multiple layers being output by the media server when the reality is that it really is just specific areas of a piece of media (commonly referred to as a clip) being positioned to fit across multiple displays.

FIGURE 16.1
Raster mapping.

These are just a few of the advantages of rendering a single piece of content from multiple clips if the intention is for playback at HD resolution. As video content being used on most productions is largely HD, the programmer has to be aware of how many layers are active at any given time, and he/she has to be creative in how those layers are physically managed.

ADDING LIVE VIDEO

Another creative use of layers involves using the live video input of a media server. Since the media server was designed

FIGURE 16.2
Raster mapping across LED curtains, Versa® TUBE, and projection screens via a single output. *Source*: Courtesy of JJ Wulf.

126

to put video at the controls of a DMX lighting console, the LD has the ability to enable a live video input at any moment. Think of this like creating a *Picture in Picture* (PiP). To set up for this, you can create a layer on top of the main image and scale it to fit within a specific area of the raster. The position and size for this layer can be saved easily on the lighting console into a palette, and you can create multiple palettes with different raster locations so that you can trigger live video on any screen in the multiple screen system at the touch of a button.[21]

As the programmer, there are many times you will be faced with challenges that require you to think outside the box. Knowing the features and limitations of your equipment will help you find creative solutions to these problems when it may appear there are none. This also means you may have to turn to additional software or documentation in order to make the pieces fit. Regardless of how it happens, the show must go on, as they say, so I say learn how to make lemonade out of lemons, and create new solutions along the way!

CHAPTER 17

Synchronizing Frames

The reality of using multiple media servers on a production is commonplace today. However, this situation has a few obstacles to overcome. In particular, synchronizing content to play simultaneously on several servers without losing sync (a condition known as *drifting*) can be a very big headache unless you use a server that allows you to sync frames between servers. Simply starting a clip and letting it roll on all servers is not going to be acceptable during a show because eventually the servers will end up showing different frames at the same time. So let's take a look at a few of the options for syncing frames between servers.

SYNCING WITHOUT A NETWORK

One method of 'syncing' multiple servers without using a network is to program a few 'reference' cues on your lighting console; these cues contain a DMX value for a specific frame of the clip. When that cue is played, all of the media servers controlled by the cue will be 'synced' again, and realigned to the same frame. If a specific frame is played at specific intervals (maybe every 20–30 seconds), then all of the media servers will appear to remain in sync with each other, and the clip will perform as expected. This is by no means the best choice for most shows, but it is one way of keeping the clip on track.

This method of using a cue to trigger a reference frame is not foolproof by any means. Although it can work in a pinch, there are a couple of things to overcome when programming a long clip. Likely the biggest headache happens when you want to jump to an earlier place in the clip. Once a clip has passed the reference frame being sent out by a cue, it is not easy to jump backward to that same reference frame as is the case when you are in rehearsals and the director says "Let's take a look at Cue 5 again." You can jump forward to another reference frame all day long, but jumping back to an earlier frame in a video clip can be problematic. A work around for this is to program a reference frame cue to a frame slightly ahead of the actual frame of the image or location in the clip (it can be as little as one frame, and therefore won't be visible to the eye). As long as the cue is referencing a frame that it hasn't yet reached, it will remain 'engaged' and will listen to the frame information from the cue.

Shifting gears slightly, I want to point out a slightly tricky situation that you will likely discover at some point when using a cue on a console to trigger a clip. That moment will be when you need to stop the movie and start again, and it occurs as you stop your cuelist on your lighting console. Simply put, the video clip will not automatically stop when you stop the lighting crossfade of a cue. Why is this? The lighting console only sends out a DMX value that corresponds to a play command on the server, and the server handles the video playback. This can present a bit of a challenge when you need to stop the clip, get reset on both the console and the server(s), and play the same cue again. In this situation, I have found a quick way to get the clip to stop and also reset to the beginning of the loop is to program a cue with the clip playback mode set to *In Frame* and the clip assigned to the first frame of the movie. Also, I recommend building this on a separate cuelist fader (using a bump button for this is actually a very effective trick) and you can use this every time you need to stop and rewind, so to speak. When you are ready to jump to a specific starting place, all that is required then is to play the cue that contains the reference frame value in your main cuelist, and the clip will immediately jump ahead to the frame of the clip.

SYNCING MEDIA SERVERS OVER A NETWORK

Syncing media servers can also be achieved over a network as well. Using a Catalyst as an example, the servers can be connected via a network, and one of the servers can be designated as the main server on the network (via its *Sync ID*). This server then sends out the master reference frame. Layers on the slave servers on the network are then assigned to listen to the same Sync ID number from the lighting console, and a video clip being played back on that layer of a slave server will then be synchronized frame by frame to the master server. An important point to stress here is that the clip itself doesn't matter. In other words, if the master server is File 1 in Library 1, a slave server doesn't have to be playing the same file to be in sync. It can actually be playing a completely different file, but the frames of each clip will still be in sync across the servers.

131

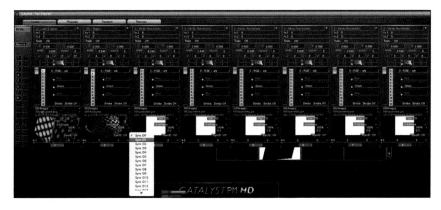

FIGURE 17.1
Catalyst Sync ID menu.

Syncing Frames to MTC

Another option for syncing frames between servers is to use MIDI timecode. In Catalyst, it is as simple as selecting a DMX value on the *Playmode* channel to assign the layer playing the video clip to listen to an incoming MTC signal. This is a great option when a click track is being used in the show because it ensures that multiple servers in the show will be in sync with the timecode consistently.[22]

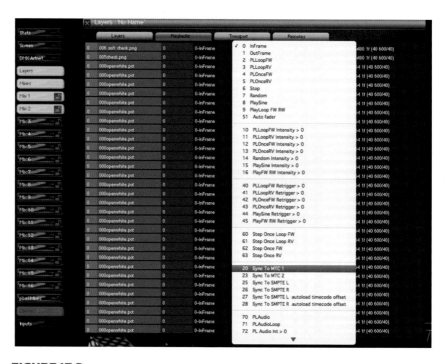

FIGURE 17.2
Catalyst MTC sync menu.

GENLOCK

Genlock refers to using a reference signal from one source to synchronize other video devices together. Genlock is commonly used in broadcast applications to ensure refresh rates between devices will all be in sync at a specific time. When Genlock is required, a generator is needed to generate the

Genlock signal (may also be referred to as *Black Burst*) that is sent to all connected display systems.

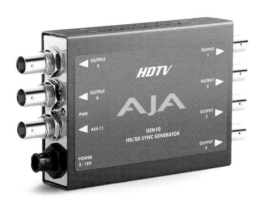

FIGURE 17.3
Genlock AJA® GEN10.

When faced with a project that requires playing a single piece of content on several servers simultaneously or segments of the same clip distributed to several servers that will be blended, it is imperative that the servers stay in sync with each other. Therefore, the use of some of these methods and the right hardware will ensure that the results will be pure synchronicity!

133

CHAPTER 18

3D Objects

Many media servers allow the programmer to take virtually any piece of content and wrap it around a 3D object. Imagine taking that corporate logo and wrapping it around a box or a banner? Suddenly, new possibilities for real-time content manipulation present themselves.

FIGURE 18.1
3D cube and teacup in Catalyst.

X, Y, Z

Every 3D object has three coordinates: X, Y, and Z. Each of these coordinates controls the physical location in space for the object. By manipulating any of these three coordinates, the object can be made to appear to change size, disappear from the screen, and even rotate around its own center point. Images may be applied to each side of the object, further creating dimension. The Mbox Extreme is a good example of a server with controls for spatial attributes like Z coordinate (depth). Take a look at Figure 18.2. In it, the objects appear to be of various sizes. In reality, however, all that is different between the three objects is the Z coordinate; the larger object is closer to the camera than the smallest object.

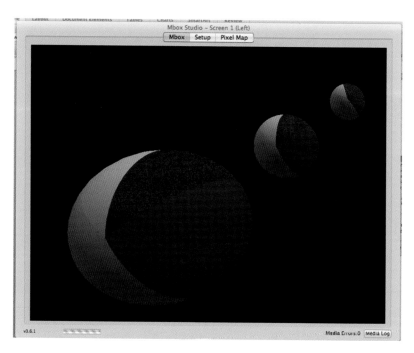

FIGURE 18.2
Spatial relationship between 3D objects in Mbox.

Many media servers also allow images to be mapped to 3D objects, so creating custom objects can be an exciting way of creating something visually unique. There are many 3D object creation applications available, and each one may have its own format. It is best to confirm the specific format required by the media server and to render the object according to the manufacturer's recommendations to ensure correct mapping and video playback.

CREATING 3D OBJECTS

Media server programmers who wish to create their own 3D objects may be able to use applications like Blender™, Cinema 4D™, Maya®, and 3DS Max™. These applications generally require additional training to use them effectively, more so than a video editing software package, but with some basic knowledge, custom 3D objects can be created and imported into most media servers. It is beyond the scope of this book to go into detail about creating advanced 3D objects, but it is important to know that creating a 3D object that allows an image to be wrapped or mapped to it requires a UV map. This UV map is literally the map that tells the server which part of the content gets mapped to which part of the object specifically. This part of the creation process can be very tedious; however, without it the object is just a plain object and images cannot be mapped to it.

Cheetah3D™ and SketchUp™ are two affordable and relatively easy to use 3D object creation applications which can also be used to create simple objects with some success. Both of these are readily available and allow objects to be created and exported in a variety of formats. SketchUp does not provide a way to edit the UV map, but the SketchUp object can be imported into Cheetah3D to create the UV map, and then exported from Cheetah3D in the desired format without issues.

137

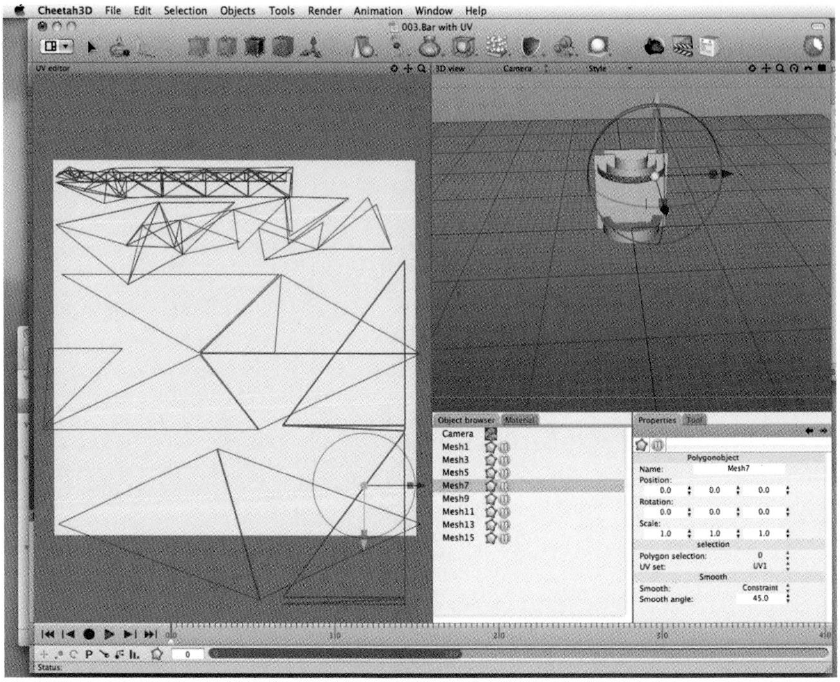

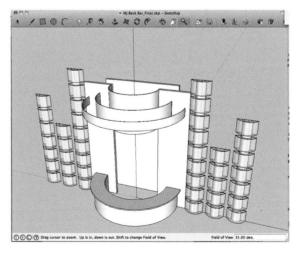

FIGURE 18.3
3D object with UV map.

FIGURE 18.4
3D object in SketchUp.

Since this area of content creation is becoming more important as servers expand capabilities, it is important not to overlook it and to learn some of the basics. However, at some point you may find yourself buried in video editing and spending less time on the console; so unless you plan to pursue a career in 3D graphics, you will likely want to hire someone to create any complex objects that you need, simply from a time/cost (and stress) perspective.

3D objects allow you to use existing content loaded on the media server, combine it with an object, and create something entirely different. While this may not be usable in every situation, it can be a fun and unique creative tool in your bag of tricks. And because it is an element of the media server, the creation happens on the server; nothing has to be pre-rendered. This means it can be viewed directly on the server with no additional time spent on content creation. How much easier can it be?

139

FIGURE 18.5
3D objects in Mbox.

CHAPTER 19

Multi-Dimensional Controls

Most media servers on the market today have some level of image distortion or surface warping controls, whether it is simply keystone correction or more advanced like spherical mapping. Some servers go beyond simply distorting the image and actually provide an interface for 3D mapping onto models. Let's take a look at several of these image distortion and mapping functions that can be used to create the illusion of 3D when using projection.

3D WARPING

Servers such as Hippotizer and Axon are frequently used in projects where an image needs to be manipulated and distorted so that it will appear flat on a curved or 3D surface. The spherical mapping features of the Axon, for instance, allow the rectangular 4:3 output from the media server to be warped across a section of a curved or irregular surface using alignment controls including latitude, longitude, vertical and horizontal center, and bend.

When using spherical mapping in a multiple projector blend, it is very helpful to project an alignment grid onto the 3D surface so that edges, sizes, and angles can be matched between each one. Once the positioning of each of the projectors has been dialed in, the centerline of the alignment grid can be aligned with the center of the 3D surface then the image can be adjusted up or down as needed. The projected grid will also be helpful for blending the image across the multiple outputs. Once edges are blended, any image selected from the library will be distributed across the multiple outputs and will be mapped to the 3D surface.

FIGURE 19.1
Spherical mapping using an Axon

HIPPOTIZER

In the Hippotizer's ScreenWarp™ Manager warps are created according to the size and/or shape of the 3D surface. Control *nodes* or handles can be added to the warp's grid and are necessary to manipulate the grid to fit on the non-linear surface. And in applications where multiple servers are being used to create the completed projected image, ScreenWarp also allows soft-edge blending around the perimeter of the warped area via controls for **Blend Left, Blend Right, Blend**

Top, and **Blend Bottom**. **Gamma** and **Overlap** controls are also available for each side of the warp and are used to create the seamless blending of adjacent warps.[23]

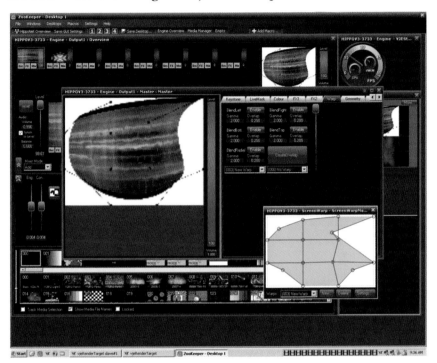

FIGURE 19.2
Image from Hippo ScreenWarp.

Below is a short list of other servers that offer similar 3D distortion controls:

- *MediaMaster Pro*: Geometric correction and geometric cylindrical distortion
- *Catalyst*: Spherical mapping and keystone correction
- *Maxedia*: Spherical projection and 3D warping
- *Mbox Designer, and Studio*: Visual distortion effects can be combined with 3D objects, keystone, and aspect ratio to create 3D warping
- *Pandoras Box*: 3D warping, 3D stereo projection, spherical projection mapping, image blending.

3D MAPPING

3D mapping differs from 3D warping in that the server actually wraps an image onto the surface of a 3D object (model) based on its UV map. Three servers available today stand apart from the field in this area; the Ai, d3, and Pandoras Box. Each of these servers allows the user to import a 3D model of the surface (e.g. a building, organic object, or other scenic element) along with its UV map into the server's virtual environment. Then the 3D model can be manipulated directly within the server and further aligned to precisely match the surface it is being projected on.

The Video Mapper extension in the ArKaos MediaMaster Pro and a standalone mapping application called MADMapper both allow you to "create" a 3D surface or object and then "simulate" the creation of a UVmap for that object in real time. The ArKaos Video Mapper does this internally within the software; MADMapper runs independently but then can accept output directly from any Syphon friendly media server (e.g. Modul8, Quartz Composer, Resolume, VDMX™).

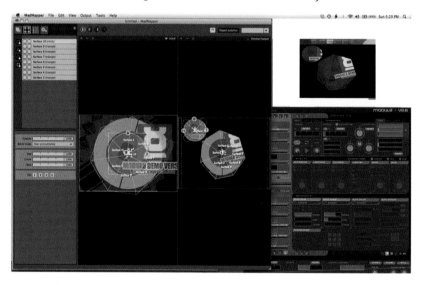

FIGURE 19.3
MADMapper and Modul8.

LARGE-SCALE STRUCTURAL MAPPING

A growing and converging market for projection and enter-tainment in recent years is in the illumination of large-scale objects and architectural structures, commonly referred to as *video mapping*. Whether the project is to celebrate an event or simply a unique way to advertise, the use of projectors fed by digital lighting media servers to illuminate the facades of buildings is one of the most rapidly growing areas of devel-opment for media servers. And in the world of electronic dance music (EDM), many DJs are creating highly sophisti-cated 3D mapping environments that completely submerge the viewer in a virtual world of real images mixed with vir-tual insanity. These images from Avicii's 2012 tour feature a 14-foot sculpted head with a podium in the forehead for the DJ himself.

FIGURE 19.4
Close-up of head from Avicii Se7en Levels Tour, 2012.

FIGURE 19.5
Setup and rehearsal, Primm NV, 2012.

For this tour, an extremely complex geometric model of the head was created in Cinema 4D and then custom content was created that was triggered by Avicii himself during the show as he mixed via a system based on Modul8 and Ableton Live™. The entire lighting and video event was locked to MIDI time-code, which allowed Avicii to change things from night to night. Other DJs including deadmau5 and Tiësto also incorporate elements of 3D media and mapping into their stage shows, and entire music festivals (e.g. Electric Daisy Carnival) have been created around dance music featuring over the top visuals, lasers, and immersive performances.

This new area of convergence between lighting and video is an exciting new way of reaching new audiences for hotels, conventions, and concerts. And with the rapid advancements in projection technology and software, this is likely to have a huge impact on advertising and productions alike.

CHAPTER 20

Pixel Mapping

Pixel mapping, as referred to in the world of digital lighting, is the use of a media server or other kind of software to map an image or video clip across a grid of LEDs and/or lighting fixtures. The image can be displayed across any type of fixture that has intensity (e.g. PAR cans). In addition to intensity, an image with color information may also be displayed across automated fixtures with RGB/CMY attributes as well (e.g. GLP Impression™ X4, Vari*Lite® VL3500™). Perhaps though, the best use of pixel mapping applications within media servers is when combined with the use of color mixing LEDs such as LED pars, LED pixel spheres, or Versa TUBE, to name a few.

FIGURE 20.1
G-Lec Solaris™ pixel spheres.

These fixtures, when grouped together in the lighting rig, essentially create a low-resolution display screen comprised of pixels of red, green, and blue LEDs that display the content being rendered by the media server. And because we are talking about digital video from the perspective of a lighting console, all of this is controllable from a lighting console.

In a standard pixel mapping system, a piece of content (still images or movie clips) is displayed across an external display of fixtures, with each fixture representing one pixel in the image. This is achieved via the mapping of the image using a pixel mapping application. The primary purpose of the application is to map the desired piece of content to the actual pixels in the display grid. Applications such as the ArKaos LED Mapper™ make this very simple. The first step usually is to start by creating a grid that will represent the maximum number of pixels that make up the image. For most non-HD applications, a grid with a low image resolution such as 640 × 480 is suitable because most LED fixtures have a limited number of pixels on the face of the fixture and will only be able to show a sort of "combined average" of the information contained in a specific area of pixels.

After setting the grid size, the next step is generally to create a pixel map which literally maps each pixel of the LED fixture to a pixel in the video image (represented by the grid). Instead of having to patch each pixel one by one, however, LED mapping applications usually contain a fixture library, very similar to a library in a lighting console. The fixture profiles in the library of the mapping application will contain the exact number and order of pixels on the fixture while also allowing these pixels to be assigned unique DMX addresses. The map, then, will be created as you add and position these library fixtures into the grid in the desired arrangement.

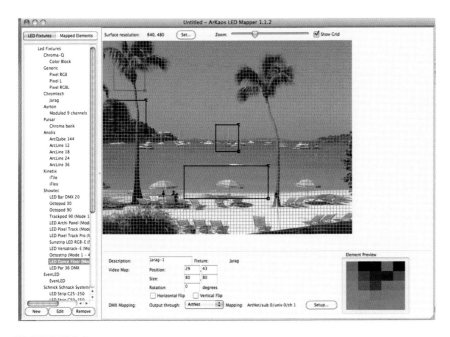

FIGURE 20.2
ArKaos LED Mapper.

149

MAPPING PIXELS

When creating a pixel map for a system, pixel flow direction is very important. Every fixture in the LED mapping application has a direction of pixel flow, in other words, a "pixel#1". If a fixture is placed out of order or placed backward in the map, the result will be that the pixels will appear wrong and the image will be incorrectly displayed. So, when adding fixtures into the map, particular attention must be given to the starting pixel on the device (is the first pixel in the device at the top, bottom, left, or right end of the fixture?). It is equally as important to confirm the order of assigned DMX addresses in order to assure correct image mapping and playback. Once all necessary fixtures have been added to the map, then the pixel information in the map will be broadcast out via Art-Net to the lighting network.

Note: somewhere in the system it may need to be converted into DMX so that it can be sent to the LED fixtures using 5-pin XLR cable.

Once the map has been created, a media server is used to create a look by selecting a piece of video content and adjusting any attributes like color, visual effect, and combining with other layers. Then, as the image is output from the server, it will be displayed across the pixels of the lighting fixtures/LEDs only showing the actual pixels according to where the fixtures were placed in the map. Again, the image displayed will not be high resolution, but this can be an extremely powerful way to provide visual energy to a stage and a much easier way of building dynamic color and movement sweeps across fixtures than building chases with the lighting console.[24]

DMX MERGE

In the situation where the fixtures that you are pixel mapping to are automated lighting fixtures with pan, tilt, gobo, shutter, and other attributes, it will be necessary to use a technique called DMX Merge. With only the RGB values of the fixtures being controlled by the media server, all other attributes of the fixture (e.g. pan, tilt, shutter) will remain controlled from the lighting console, so those two separate streams of data will have to be combined (merged) back together in the system. There are boxes available to do this (Doug Fleenor's DMX Combine is one example), as well as consoles (grandMA2) and power/data distribution systems (PRG's Series400). The concept sounds complex, but as long as you have the right gear in the system to do the merging, it really is not difficult.

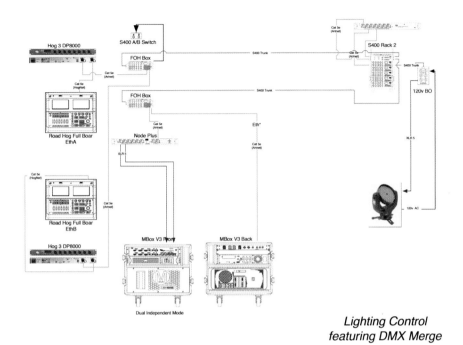

*Lighting Control
featuring DMX Merge*

FIGURE 20.3
DMX Merge diagram.

151

PIXEL MAPPING CONTROL

Most media servers have a pixel mapping control interface, and they pretty much have the same purpose: to assign a pixel of an image to the intensity and/or color of an LED or automated fixture. Some lighting consoles are also beginning to incorporate pixel mapping and bitmap mapping engines into their workflow to better assist the lighting programmer when working with digital lighting. Two of these, the ChamSys MagicQ and the grandMA2, feature onboard pixel mapping engines.

The Pixel Mapper engine in the ChamSys MagicQ allows a piece of media content from a media server to be mapped to a grid of pixels using the **Media** window directly on the console. You start by creating a grid wherein each pixel in the grid will represent a fixture or an LED in a fixture. Once the grid has been created, you assign a *Pixelmap Engine* to the grid:

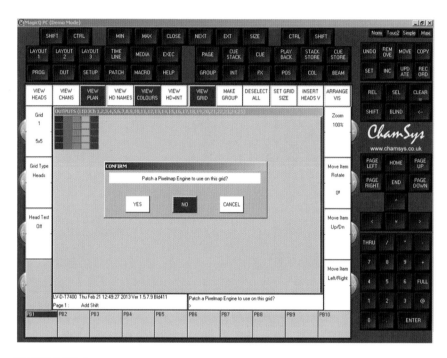

FIGURE 20.4
ChamSys MagicQ pixelmap engine.

After an engine is assigned to the grid, then the engine will appear in the media window alongside other media servers, and once selected, it allows you to choose any piece of media to playback on the grid.

The thumbnail in the window indicates how the video will be mapped to the grid. This set up works best if you are using a media server that can communicate with the ChemSys MagicQ via CITP so that the actual videos appear in the media window. ChemSys MagicQ does also have an onboard bitmap FX engine though, if you do not have a

FIGURE 20.5
ChamSys MagicQ pixelmap engine media window.

media server but still want something dynamic to be displayed on your wall of Jarags™ or LEDs.

Moving on to the grandMA2, this console features an onboard *Bitmap Effects Engine* that currently includes bitmaps of just about every gobo available. It also allows you to upload your own custom bitmap into the console as well. Once a bitmap has been chosen, dynamic waveforms can be applied to create motion, as well as scale, rotation, and position movement effects. Again, this works well in situations where you want a little something more than just a color chase or intensity chase across your LEDs.

When using an external media server with the grandMA2 (not the grandMA VPU), you will generally build a pixel map in the media server, then output the DMX values of the content mapped to that pixel map directly to the digital lighting fixtures. The console simply triggers the cue which in turn triggers the media server to play a certain video.

FIGURE 20.6
grandMA2 bitmap effects engine.

As lighting continues to merge with video, pixel mapping is becoming a frequently used effect for lighting designers. With all the LED products on the market, the knowledge of pixel mapping is rapidly becoming the norm. Fortunately, lighting consoles continue to evolve, and more tools and features are being developed to help the lighting programmer manage all of the additional channels of DMX control for all of these LEDs and media servers.

CHAPTER 21

Using Audio with Media Servers

Occasionally when programming with a media server you will be asked if the media server can output audio because the client would like to use a clip that also contains audio. This is not a difficult process for most media servers, but there are a few things to be familiar with when using a media server's audio output.

INTERNAL CONTROL

Many media servers support audio output, and typically the server will be enabled or disabled via a channel within the DMX protocol, so it can easily be turned on or off for each clip as needed. For some servers though, a different method of enabling audio may be required, as is the case for MBox Designer. When a file that contains audio is loaded in the Mbox, the label must contain an additional bit of information ("001.myvideo.*audio*.mov") in order for the Mbox to understand that it can play the audio portion when the video is triggered. Because no two servers operate identically, it is always recommended to refer to the user manual for the specific requirements.

HARDWARE

Most media servers come with a factory installed sound card, and the output connector on that audio card is usually referred to as a *mini-jack*, or 1/8-inch mini-jack.

FIGURE 21.1
Mini-jack.

These connectors are very common on most consumer electronic devices on the market, and they will almost always be in stereo. *Note*: some media servers feature additional audio ports for use with professional audio systems. Mbox Designer, for instance, has built in 3-pin XLR balanced left and right audio out ports on the rear of its IO module.

Some additional common cables and connectors that you may likely encounter or need when working with audio are:

FIGURE 21.2
RCA.

FIGURE 21.3
TRS.

FIGURE 21.4
3-pin XLR.

While we're on the topic of XLR cable, do you know the difference between a 3-pin XLR cable used for audio and a 3-pin XLR cable used for DMX? They are not the same! Many people will say that it is ok to use an audio XLR cable for DMX, and in some situations where the distance between console and fixtures is short, an audio XLR cable may work in a pinch. The operative word here is "may." Physically, the 3-pin XLR cable that is labeled as a DMX cable is rated at 120 ohms and is used to transmit a digital signal whereas an audio XLR cable is rated at 80 ohms and is used to transmit an analog signal. What this means is that on longer runs, an XLR DMX cable can transmit the signal further than an audio XLR cable with less signal loss. And cleaner signal means fewer problems with fixtures freaking out in the rig. Thus, you should always make sure that you use an audio XLR cable for audio and an XLR DMX cable for lighting.

STEREO OR MONO

Another important detail to mention is whether a mini-jack or TRS connector is stereo or mono. Simply put, a mono connector only transmits the audio signal down one channel (the left), while stereo transmits audio down both channels (left and right). The easiest way to tell one from the other is whether it has two insulating rings on the tip (stereo) or only one (mono). Figure 21.1 is an example of a stereo connector, while Figure 21.3 is an example of a mono connector. Make sure you have the right adapters so you can easily adapt from one type of connector to another as needed.

No matter the media server you're using, always consult the user manual for the recommended audio formats for the server. Just like formats for video, not all servers use the same format for audio.

CHAPTER 22

Timecode, MIDI, and TouchOSC

When it comes to show control, a media server will likely have many options. These options usually involve a show controller that triggers the server via one of the following options:

- Timecode (SMPTE, MTC)
- MIDI Notes (MIDI)
- TouchOSC™.

TIMECODE

Using timecode for show control does not take the place of programming with the server. In other words, if you are not using a lighting console to program the cues, then you will need to use either an internal timeline or an external proprietary application to create and store the video cues. Then the timecode stamp can be added to the cue directly in the timeline on the server or proprietary application that will allow that cue to be triggered when it reaches the timecode stamped on the cue. Yes, I am speaking in very broad terms here because when it comes to timecode, every server has a different method of implementation. Since it is not possible to cover how to set up timecode or MIDI for every server in this book, I would like to point out a few basic things about using timecode and MIDI that could be helpful while programming.

Most major lighting consoles feature an internal timecode simulator feature. This is very helpful, especially when you are pre-programming without the actual timecode source being present. My first suggestion is to program every cue you think you need in any specific section first, then if the console has a **Learn Timing** (e.g. WholeHog 4) feature, turn on the **Learn Timing** button while a simulated timecode is being generated by the console and start pressing the **Go** button on the cuelist for each cue. This is an easy way to stamp a simulated timecode onto each cue, and then these time stamps can be easily edited once the actual timecode source is connected to the console. You can also use this learn timing method when the actual timecode source is present. Be prepared for a lot of tweaking once timecode has been stamped however; it takes a lot of **Play**, **Stop**, **Rewind** to get a cue to fire the exact moment that you need it.

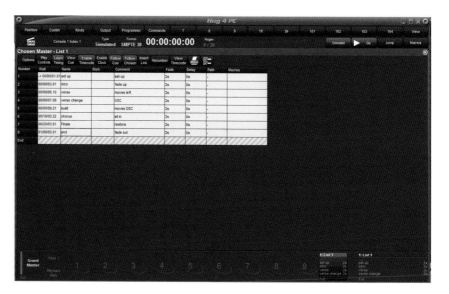

FIGURE 22.1
Hog4®PC cuelist with timecode.

The biggest drawback to cueing with videos is that timecode will only trigger the cue that plays the video clip, so if you stop the timecode, it does not stop the video clip. Therefore, as I mentioned in Chapter 17, I recommend creating a single cue on a different fader or handle that changes the play mode to stop and resets the movie back to frame 1; then when timecode starts again, the file will be triggered and advanced to the correct frame.

If you are using an Mbox Designer, you will be able to synchronize a video file directly to timecode without the need for a cuelist. This is because the Mbox application allows you to put the timecode value directly into the label of the cue (the label would look something like "001.mymovie. TC-02-12-14-07.mov", and then via the MBox Remote application, timecode sent to the server will not only trigger the correct file, but also, when the file is stopped or scrubbed to another frame, the file on the MBox will follow. The drawback of using this method of timecode sync is that the file has to be pre-rendered with all desired effects because it is only triggering a file, not a lighting cue. This could be very useful though in applications where a few videos are simply triggered at various times of the day as in a trade show booth or installation because it eliminates the need for a console and an operator.

161

MIDI NOTES

Not all professional touring servers have implemented MIDI Notes, but this is becoming more readily available as the popularity of electronic dance music and visual DJ software increases. For instance, the ArKaos GrandVJ® software was designed from the beginning to operate via MIDI. The programmer starts by creating a mapping template that essentially maps a specific control channel or feature of the ArKaos software to a specific physical button on a MIDI controller. A virtually endless number of customized setups can be created and saved for working with practically any MIDI device. Some of the popular MIDI controllers used by visual DJs include the Numark® NuVJ™ Video Mixer, M-Audio®'s Axiom™ and Oxygen™ controllers, SmithsonMarten®'s Emulator™, and Codanova's VMX™ VJ, to get you started.

FIGURE 22.2
MIDI cables.

TOUCH OSC

The visual DJ, or as the industry has renamed it the "VJ", now has an additional option for a control interface known as TouchOSC. TouchOSC, created by Hexlar, was developed for iPhone®, iPad®, and iPod Touch®. It allows the user to create custom templates that map buttons and encoders on the interface to functions in the media server software. TouchOSC is powerful because it allows you to connect to practically any MIDI capable application via one of three methods:

- Open Sound Control (OSC)
- MIDI Bridge
- Core MIDI.[25]

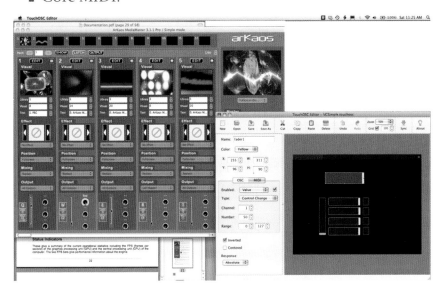

FIGURE 22.3
TouchOSC control template for ArKaos MediaMaster Pro.

Using MIDI to control video can be a lot of fun, especially in a live music venue or dance club, and it is definitely more interactive than programming every cue on a lighting console; but it does require organization and more than anything else—creativity! The VJ, after all, is a performer who is a vital part of the performance. And with tools like these, you will be able to show off your brightest ideas!

CHAPTER 23

The Evolution of Media Servers

As media servers evolve, more are beginning to offer methods for controlling the software without using a lighting console. These methods, either internally or via a separate application, open the door to a wider range of technicians who are not familiar with how to program a lighting console or who simply do not understand DMX, but who want to be able to take advantage of some of the real-time manipulation of video that media servers allow (e.g. layering a corporate logo over a moving image background).

While there are some pros for controlling a server via DMX, such as being able to apply effects from the lighting console's effects engine to create endless variations of the same clip, the programming interface can be quite complex and the number of DMX channels required can be extremely high. Programming a media server in this fashion requires good organizational skills as well as a lot of presets, palettes, and groups to be able to effectively manage the numerous layers, effects, and objects that make up a real-time compositing media server. So it can be very appealing to a video engineer who understands media but not lighting consoles to have an alternative method of using a media server.

These non-DMX based control interfaces vary in their approach, but most typically provide a format for creating scenes, storing the scenes, and triggering the scenes manually or via a timeline or cuelist.

TIMELINES

Media servers with internal playback control may provide this control via a timeline feature. Scenes can be created directly on the server using the user interface and then stored into a timeline that can be triggered either manually or remotely using timecode.

- Hippotizer

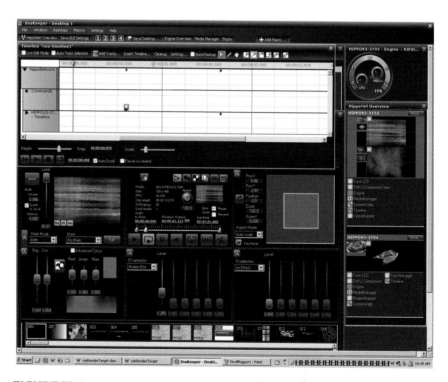

FIGURE 23.1
Hippotizer timeline.

■ Pandoras Box

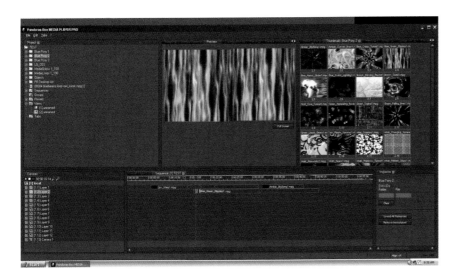

FIGURE 23.2
Pandoras Box timeline.

■ PlaybackPro™

FIGURE 23.3
Playback Pro timeline.

PRESETS, CUES, AND CUELISTS

Instead of using a timeline, some media servers allow stored cues or presets to be played back directly from the user interface via a computer keyboard, mouse, or touchscreen. These server applications offer direct access to the playback of these stored looks in any order instead of a determined sequence, making these interfaces a bit more flexible for a live event such as dance music festivals as well as corporate shows that may involve unrehearsed music or other material.

- ArKaos MediaMaster Pro

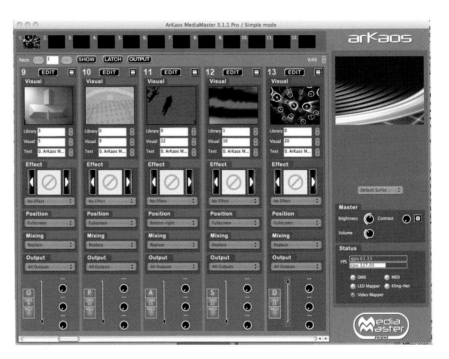

FIGURE 23.4
ArKaos MediaMaster Pro simple mode.

- Maxedia

FIGURE 23.5
Maxedia Cue AB window.

- Catalyst

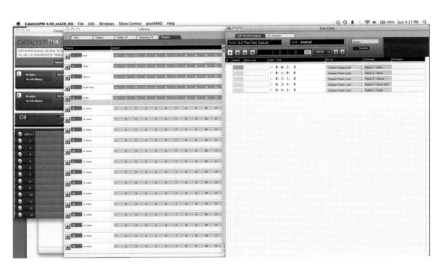

FIGURE 23.6
Catalyst cuelist.

STAND-ALONE APPLICATIONS

A separate stand-alone application is typically written as a proprietary piece of software that works specifically with a certain server or brand of servers. Most applications for this type of control either run directly on the same server or are connected via a network while running on an external computer. Mbox Director, for instance, is a stand-alone application that is used to store cues for playback without a console, but it can also be used to control media on multiple Mbox servers.

FIGURE 23.7
Mbox Director timeline.

Tip: if the application can run on an external computer and you can network to the server, then it is a good idea to use this method for a couple of reasons. First, it does not take away processing power from the server application, and secondly, if the control application freezes or stops working, the server doesn't stop working.

There are many advantages for controlling a media server using one of these methods instead of via DMX. One is that these user interfaces are designed in such a way that it is easier to locate all of a server's features rather than having to use a DMX channel to dial up a specific value. Another advantage is that they may feature thumbnails and/or streaming video for previewing the media. These features make interacting with an otherwise complex software application very manageable and accessible. If you are not as familiar with lighting consoles or DMX, or you just simply do not want to use a lighting console for a simple type of show, these and many more options for control are available.

CHAPTER 24

Inside a Virtual Environment

A 2D media server simply plays back digital content as if projected on a flat surface. A 3D media server, on the other hand, creates a virtual 3D environment in real time using a combination of layers and objects.

The Ai and d3 servers go even further into the 3D world by creating a 3D space. The programmer is able to load in a full 3D model of any object and use the screen to program directly on the surface. Figure 24.1 shows how a 3D sphere is configured in the Stage Construction page of the Ai.

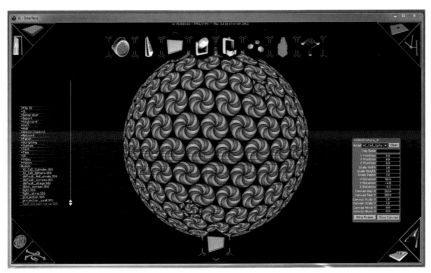

FIGURE 24.1
3D object in Ai.

Simulating pixel mapping across a complex object such as a curved LED wall is also possible in these media servers, as seen in Figure 24.2.

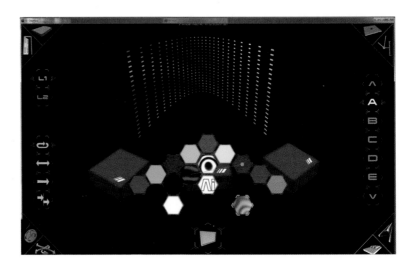

FIGURE 24.2
Curved LED screen in Ai.

Not only do Ai and d3 allow the programmer to see the object being manipulated, full scale models of venues can be imported as well, making these servers powerful visualizers for pre-programming similar to a program like WYSIWYG, ESP Vision, or Capture™ Polar Light Converse™.

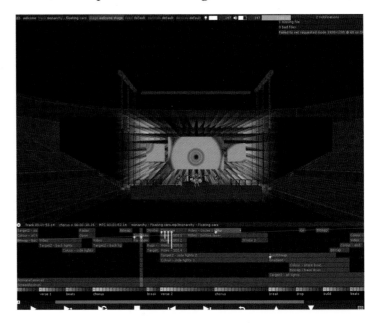

FIGURE 24.3
d3 stage view.

Sophisticated media servers such as Ai and d3 create virtual worlds that can be incredibly useful for programming. With the use of these types of virtual environments, the entire show can literally be programmed ahead of time. Both Ai and d3 feature timelines that allow cues to be created directly in the server in a similar fashion to a show control application.

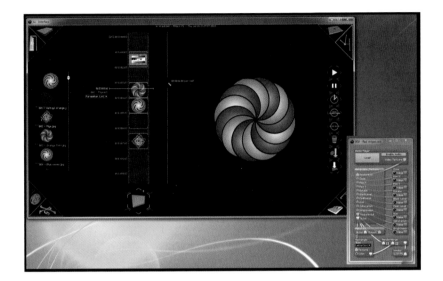

FIGURE 24.4
Ai timeline.

175

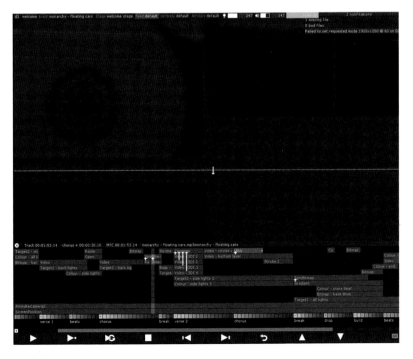

FIGURE 24.5
d3 timeline.

These cues can trigger audio files and lighting fixtures as well as the video clips, and then the resulting 'show' can be rendered, exported, and sent off to the client for approval. Considering the pre-production period for video can be months long, this means that everyone can see the finished product long before show day, and once onsite, the only programming that will remain is adjustments to location of projectors in the model to match where they are located in the real world. Using these types of servers can definitely save time and money but they also open the door to more possibilities in the large-scaled architectural mapping events.

CHAPTER 25

DMX Controlled Digital Lighting

An important part in the convergence of lighting and video is the evolution of DMX controlled projectors. With the increasing use of media servers on productions, many designers not only want to control a production's video content from a lighting desk, they want to have control over how and where that image is being projected. This is where digital lighting fixtures like High End Systems' DML-1200™, DL.3, and DLV™ can be very useful.

FIGURE 25.1
Left to right: DML-1200, DL.3, DLV.

WHY USE A DIGITAL MOVING LIGHT?

Lighting designers who find themselves in the role of visual director for a show will oversee all visual elements of the production ranging from scenic to video to lighting. In some cases, a high output projector that is fixed onto a static location may be all that is required for the production. However, a digital moving light can be easily controlled from a DMX lighting console and using one gives the designer the freedom to focus the projector onto various surfaces in multiple locations while simplifying the creation process.

UNDERSTANDING THE TOOLS

Digital lighting luminaires have a wide range of features, and their ideal applications are varied as a result. Let's take a look at some of the earliest products available on the digital lighting market.

DL.1 by High End Systems

The Icon M launched an entirely new line of lighting fixtures. One of the more popular fixtures to evolve after the Icon M was retired was the DL.1®. The DL.1 started as a digital projector built into a housing supported by a yoke that could pan and tilt. The DL.1 did not have an onboard media server, and required a video input from a video source and/ or media server for its image projection. The unit itself was controlled via DMX, and the channels included pan, tilt, shutter, remote focus and zoom of the projector lens, and an optional camera.

DL.2 by High End Systems

The DL.2 evolved from the DL.1 and became the first digital luminaire with an onboard media server (which was also eventually released as a separate stand-alone product known as the Axon Media Server). In addition to a variety of channels for controlling over 65,000 media files, the DL.2 server also featured channels for remotely controlling the focus and zoom of the DL.2's onboard camera as well as the mode of the camera.

DL.3 by High End Systems

The DL.3 carried on the DL lineage with improvements in output, additional visual effects, advanced 3D mapping controls, and SDI inputs.

Robe DigitalSpot DT™

Robe also entered the digital lighting arena in the mid-2000s with the DigitalSpot DT line. These are primarily used in Europe and have only had a minimal presence in the United States to date. Fixtures in the DigitalSpot DT line feature an onboard media server with two digital gobo layers, each with 255 images, and control channels for XYZ rotate, scale, and indexing.

FIGURE 25.2
Robe DS7000™.

Orbital Heads and Projector Yokes

High End Systems' ArenaView™ Orbital Head and Christie® Digital's Nitro Solutions range of projector/moving yoke combinations allow media server technology to be used in applications including televised sporting events and large-scale entertainment arenas. Christie's projector/moving yoke units provide the flexibility of using any media server with a wide range of Christie projectors ranging in output from 5k to 20k while High End Systems' ArenaView allows for both the flexibility to choose the media server as well as the projector.[26]

FIGURE 25.3
ArenaView Orbital Head.

This chapter would not be complete without mentioning something obvious: these are lighting fixtures, and they can be used in all of the same applications where you would or might need a hard-edged gobo fixture. The main difference between a digital lighting fixture and a fixture with a gobo is the ability to play video instead of shining light through a pattern. But, for those applications where you may need the traditional gobos as well, some servers include as stock content the gobo catalogs from companies such as Rosco®, DHA®, and Apollo®. If not, then you can usually create your own gobo as an image file and upload it to the server.

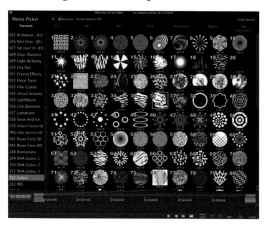

FIGURE 25.4
Stock gobo library.

Understanding the differences between these digital lighting fixtures will help you decide which one is right for your production. One size definitely does not fit all applications!

CHAPTER 26

LED Display Devices

In this chapter we will take a closer look at how video can be integrated into a production using LED technology. LEDs have allowed scenic, lighting, and video designers to incorporate video elements into all aspects of a live performance in ways previously not possible.

INNOVATIVE TECHNOLOGY

The innovations in LED technology have resulted in some exciting lighting fixtures for the entertainment industry. Why is this? To start, LEDs have many advantages over discharge and incandescent sources. Some of the advantages of LEDs include:

- Long lamp life (25,000–50,000 hours)
- Economic benefits—because there are no lamps to replace, this also means there are no associated labor costs involved
- Lower maintenance costs because of the fixture's limited moving parts—this reduces the total cost of ownership as compared to traditional lighting fixtures
- Low energy consumption.

FIGURE 26.1
Close-up of LEDs.

Manufacturers of entertainment lighting have lately been focusing on building LED wash fixtures for all of these reasons. Many challenges, specifically brightness, have led to technological advancements in the LEDs themselves as well as optics and microprocessing chips. The result is several types of fixtures that are comparable to traditional lighting fixtures but with added features, including:

- LED color wash fixtures
- Lo-res graphics LED fixtures.

LED COLOR WASH FIXTURES

These moving yoke LED fixtures are strictly color wash fixtures, and video images cannot be mapped to the individual LEDs in their display. One of the best examples of this type of LED fixture is the GLP Impression 120 RZ.

FIGURE 26.2
GLP Impression 120 RZ.

LO-RES GRAPHICS LED FIXTURES

High End Systems introduced designers to a new term *Pixelation Luminaires*™ which was coined to describe their hybrid LED lo-res graphics/wash fixtures. These fixtures were a cross between a high power LED wash light and a fully programmable motion graphic display fixture capable of displaying lo-res visual images and effects. The High End Systems' ShowPix® featured a circular array of 127 LEDs. The smaller StudioPix® offered the same flexibility on a smaller scale with a circular array of 61 LEDs.[27]

FIGURE 26.3
StudioPix and ShowPix.

Similar low-resolution LED yoke fixtures have been released since HES launched the ShowPix, in a variety of shapes and sizes, including the MagicPanel™ 602 from Ayrton.

FIGURE 26.4
MagicPanel 602. *Source*: Photo courtesy of Valere Huart of Ayrton.

CREATIVE LED TECHNOLOGY

New LED technology is being introduced in many shapes and sizes. Even strobes and audience blinders have been updated. For example, the ELAR Quad™ Panels from Elation, the Nexus™ 4×4 from Chauvet, and the Eurolite®16×30w COB Performance Cluster from Eurolite are all fixed lo-res LED panels with color mixing and pixel mapping capability and a lot of output, making them very attractive and practical for lighting designers and scenic designers alike.

FIGURE 26.5
Elation ELAR Quad Panels.

FIGURE 26.6
Eurolite 16×30w Performance Clusters.

The individual LEDs on each of these types of hybrid lighting/video panels can be accessed via DMX, making them ideal for pixel mapping applications. This means that not only can you get a big blast of light in any color you want without having to use gel scrollers, you can pixel map an image across these panels using practically any media server.

In 2013 Philips introduced its Philips Showline Nitro 510 LED strobe that not only has an output of over 68,000 lumens, it allows the pixels on the face of the strobe to be pixel mapped across six regions (see Figure 26.7), making this a truly unique strobe that can be included in the pixel mapping of an entire stage.

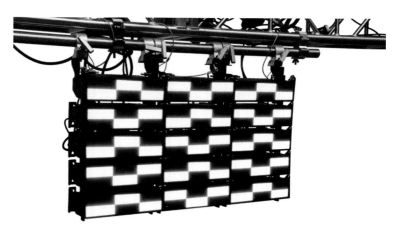

FIGURE 26.7
Philips® Showline™ Nitro 510™ LED Strobe.

Pixel mapping is not limited to LEDs. Companies such as Chromlech and Elements have re-introduced LDs to the fun of pixel mapping with low-voltage fixtures in recent years with products including Jarag-5™, Elidy™, and the Krypton Kr25™. These are essentially fixtures with a matrix of dimmable lamps that allow access to each circuit via DMX. While they do not change color, they do allow graphics to be displayed, making them a more exciting tool than a standard 3-circuit audience blinder.

FIGURE 26.8
Jarag-5 Par30. *Source:* Courtesy of ACT Lighting.

SCENIC ALTERNATIVES

Scenic designers are faced with many options for creating a set, and many scenic designers are embracing LED technology into various elements around the stage. One of the original LED fixtures commonly used in scenic designs that also helped bridge the gap between LED lighting and video is the Barco Versa TUBE. Originally launched in 2004 by Element Labs, the Versa TUBE has been one of the most successful products from their line of video display products, which also included Versa®TILE.

FIGURE 26.9
Versa TUBEs in action. *Source:* Courtesy of John Monaco.

The Versa TUBE features a row of 36 pixels composed of red, green, and blue LEDs. Instead of just mixing solid colors, though, these LEDs can be pixel mapped via the D2 processor so you get moving colors, patterns, and dynamic visual effects.

Innovative LED lighting/video products are continually being developed and feature unique shapes and configurations. Some examples of these types of out of the ordinary products include:

- G-LEC+ Solaris 360° degree Pixel Sphere Curtain
- PixelFLEX® LED Curtain
- SGM® LT-100™ LED Pixel Tubes.

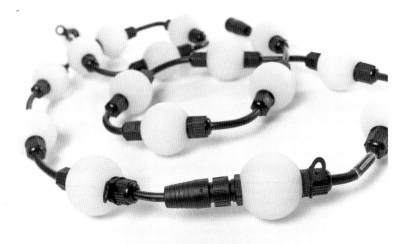

FIGURE 26.10
Solaris + 360° pixel spheres.

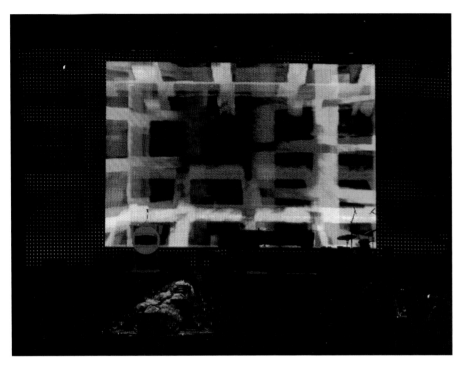

FIGURE 26.11
PixelFLEX LED 20 mm and 100 mm Curtains.

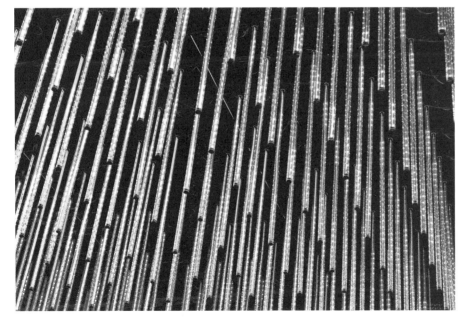

FIGURE 26.12
SGM® LT-100™/LT-200™ Pixel Tube.

These products represent some of the most creative and versatile implementations of LEDs available in the current digital lighting market. Many designers have discovered that a single fixture with multiple LEDs can be more versatile than a single point source, because it can be used to create many looks from one basic design without drastically increasing the budget. For this reason (as well as a few others like cost), lighting manufacturers continue to design fixtures based on this versatility which in turn gives the designers new tools that are capable of dynamic and unique visual effects.

Conclusion

EMBRACING NEW TECHNOLOGY

While most lighting designers and programmers may not start out working with video, in today's world of entertainment it is more than likely that at some point a media server project will present itself. And it's at that moment that you as that designer and/or programmer have the opportunity to expand both your skills and your creativity, should you choose to embrace the opportunity. With just a basic foundation of the types of concepts that have been presented in this book, you will be better prepared to take on that project with confidence. So grab your board, hop on the technology wave, and start surfing! As long as you stay ready and prepared for brand new challenges along the way, you'll find a whole new world of creativity that you never knew existed ... inside you!

FIGURE A1.1
Aria NYE 2012. *Source:* Courtesy of Kelly McKeon.

Over the last few years I have kept working journals and filled them with a-ha moments, thoughts, and questions during pre-production for several large private New Year's Eve events at a major resort in Las Vegas. I thought it would be helpful to share the process of content creation and preparation that I typically follow for these shows. Here is a compilation of those notes; I hope you find them useful.

THREE MONTHS UNTIL SHOW

Pre-production meetings and design revisions begin and are ongoing. The meetings are always driven by budget refinements, but they are always creative, and everyone throws out every conceivable variation of the concept until we all decide what the direction will be.

These shows are always content heavy and we usually use no less than three or four media servers at a time to control video for a variety of LED fixtures and/or panels as well as projections screens. Over the last couple of years, pixel mapping and video mapping have increasingly been added into these shows, and in 2012 the scenic design included several 90 foot wide 3D mapping structures inside the ballroom. Since these NYE shows are over four hours long, I have to spend a large amount of time sourcing, gathering, and preparing the video content that will be shown in the room during the night. And for highly customized content, I have many discussions both with the producer and director as well as the content creation staff (if needed) in order to make sure the visuals used during the evening are as exciting and perfect as possible.

When I discuss projects like these, usually the first question that I get asked is "How do you pick content for the event?" This is likely the most subjective part of the preparation. I use my instinct, my gut, my 'inner voice' … in other words, I pick a large percentage of the content by feel. However, it's not a guessing game. In order to come to the place where I have a sense of what is needed, I ask myself things like, "What is the theme of the party? What colors are in the scenery and décor of the room? What kind of music will be playing? Are there any highlighted production numbers that need specific images or types of video content? What are the costumes for each piece?" Once I have some general information like this, I can begin searching for inspiration.

Another critically important thing I do is listen. I listen to the scenic designer. I listen to the choreographer. I listen to the producer. I listen to the director. I want to absorb as much of their input as possible so that I can give them exactly what they are looking for.

The creative part of the process of finding the right content for a four-hour plus NYE party for 2 000 plus people begins by listening to the musical tracks of the production numbers. These parties typically have 10 production numbers with 15–20 minutes of live music in between each section. So a lot of fresh content is always required.

As I listen to the music, I try to identify the tempo, color, and energy that might fit each piece. If I'm not able to find a piece of stock content that works on the server, then I turn to the web to take a quick look at the artist's video, especially if the song isn't sending me any really clear images. While watching the videos, I make notes on anything that catches my eye: shadow, patterns, theme, etc. From these words I usually form a direction that I want to build on for each piece. If it's an electronic dance piece, for instance, then I will likely want content that reflects that style and try to create something that works with the feel and tempo of the music. This is a very creative part of the process and is very subjective as well. It is also the part that usually meets with the most resistance, especially if the artist or director has something different in mind. Each choice I make is subject to the final approval of these people, but most importantly the approval of the producer, as it's his or her vision of the show that I'm trying to create. So it's best to run ideas past the important parties before spending too much time on one idea only to be shot down.

TWO MONTHS UNTIL SHOW

After I have gathered everyone's input, my notes, and my thoughts about the overall style of the show, I then sit down

197

with the content I chose and/or created for the event. Once all the content has been created, which can take weeks or months to search for and compile, if not being created specifically, I will spend some time transcoding it to the proper format and codec if necessary (which is usually always). This may take some time as well, so I try to give myself plenty of time ahead to get this part done. And it's tedious as well, so I usually try to have some good music playing to keep from dying of boredom.

ONE MONTH UNTIL SHOW

After the content is encoded properly, I have to organize it and assemble it all into folders that I create and label by song or performance. Inside each folder I like to number and label the content in order of how it will be used in the performance as well. This makes searching for the clip faster on site, especially if all I have in front of me is a lighting console.

Once all of the content is organized, the next step is to load it all onto the media server. Since media files can be quite large, this is best to do overnight or when I can work on something else while the server is tied up. So I drag the file into the media files directory on the server and then leave it. Later (or the next morning) when I return, hopefully the content has been transferred successfully and the server is ready to go.[28]

The next step happens when I arrive on site and finish setting up FOH. That's when I can begin experimenting with the content while giving attention to what works and what doesn't. If a piece doesn't work, I may try affecting it with a visual effect or adding color until I find something that I feel fits. If however it doesn't work, I simply skip it and move on.

I like to start out with the set list and then program a simple cue into the lighting console for each song that also contains the information for the media server. Then I sculpt my lighting look around that video's energy and color until I feel like they match. And that's how I begin. While this is of course just the beginning of the programming work to be done, it allows me to get my thoughts out of my head and onto the stage. From there, my creative right brain takes over and the rest is purely subjective.

NIGHT OF SHOW

On the big night, if I have done all of my preparation and programming, then I can sit behind the console with the confidence of knowing I am ready for any surprises that may come up. And they do, always. Whether it's the band playing songs out of order or simply the producer cutting a number from the show, it pays to be prepared by having some generic looks available on a stand-by cuestack handle. This allows me to be able to transition in and out of any unforeseen problem areas in the show. I also like to have some quick access flash buttons with visual effects stored and accessible for adding some live spice to the mix when the party cranks up at 12:01 a.m.

And possibly the most important tip of all I can share is this: once the party ends, don't forget to thank your crew. Without each and every one of them, you wouldn't get to do what you get to do.

Now, erase all that content off all those servers before you pack them up!

Appendix B
Common
Troubleshooting

Below are some common issues that may arise when working with a media server.

CONTENT RELATED ISSUES

- Symptom: video won't play or plays but with unexpected problems
  Solution: wrong codec, wrong resolution, wrong format, or simply file may be too large for the GPU to process efficiently. Re-formatting with a different codec may be the best solution.
- Symptom: video looks pixelated
  Solution: possibly low resolution source material, or image is scaled at a higher resolution than the content was created at, causing the pixels to be stretched. Try reducing the amount of scale being applied to the image, or find a higher resolution image.
- Symptom: video shows jagged rips, tears
  Solution: poor source material or formatted incorrectly upon rendering export; re-render the content if possible.
- Symptom: content has horizontal lines when played back
  Solution: content is interlaced; solution is to de-interlace and reimport into server.

HARDWARE RELATED ISSUES

- Symptom: computer boots into black screen
  Solution: application may have booted into FullScreen or Show Ready mode; exit this mode to access controls.

- Symptom: GUI appears on wrong output

  Solution: likely the DVI device that was supposed to be connected to the GUI was incorrectly connected to a different output or not present at all. To correct this, connect all DVI devices before booting up computer if possible. Then turn on the server, open the Displays settings in the control panel and configure the windows so that the GUI is reconfigured to appear on the correct output.

- Symptom: media "drifts" during playback and doesn't play in sync with other layers or servers

  Solution: syncing the layers or servers via layer sync, frame sync, timecode, or genlock will correct this issue and keep all layers/servers in sync.

- Sympton: audio doesn't stay in sync with video during playback.

  Solution: there can be many reasons for this, but one of the primary reasons is that the GPU is struggling to process the file either because the file is formatted incorrectly, the audio codec is not a preferred codec, or even that the file is simply too large for the GPU to process. Always follow the recommended codec settings to better help the GPU work more efficiently.

NETWORKING ISSUES

- Sympton: multiple servers are connected but not communicating or not seeing each other

  Solution: check the IP addresses of all computers and assign each within the same IP range.

- Symptom: video thumbnails and/or live streaming videos aren't appearing on console or in a remote viewing application

  Solution: confirm that the console and/or remote viewing application has video thumbnails or streaming functionality. If so, check that all settings have been enabled and configured on both the server and the console or remote computer and a valid IP address has been assigned to all devices on the same network. Last but not least, read the user manual for exact setup for the specific devices you are configuring because each device may have unique steps for enabling this functionality.

■ Sympton: when setting up Art-Net to control a media server, the lighting console doesn't have control of the server

Solution: check that a valid Art-Net IP address has been assigned to each device on the network. All Art-Net addresses will also have to be within the same IP range and subnet range. Last but not least, confirm that the lighting console's outputs are configured correctly for communication and for sending Art-Net.

Appendix C
Glossary

Below is some common terminology you may encounter when working with media servers.

3D Mapping   The process for aligning a 2D image on a 3D object.

3D Object   An object with three dimensions (height, width, and depth). Can be physical object or virtual object created with software.

Alpha Channel   Each pixel in an image can contain four channels of information: channels for red, green, and blue, as well as the alpha channel, which stores transparency information.

Artifact   Any undesired distortion in an image that is visible while the image is being viewed.

Art-Net   A communication protocol created by Artistic License for sending multiple universes of DMX-512 over an Ethernet network.

Aspect Ratio   A ratio between the width and height of an image.

Bitrate   Refers to how much data is measured passing a specific point over a specific length of time.

Blocking   An artifact that can occur when compressed media is decompressed incorrectly; it appears as a large distorted block of pixels.

BNC   An acronym for Bayonet Neill-Concelman. This style of connector is commonly used in video cables like SDI and coaxial cables.

Brightness   Refers to how much light an image appears to give off. This is primarily a subjective measurement and may also be referred to as the *black level* of an image.

Candela   The measurement of luminous intensity approximately equal to the luminous intensity emitted by one candle.

Chroma Key   The most common example is the green screen effect; a specific color (chroma) in a foreground image is designated to be transparent, allowing another layer of video in the background to become visible.

CITP   An acronym for Controller Interface Transport Protocol; protocol that enables communication between lighting consoles, media servers, and programming visualizers and allows for the sharing of media thumbnails or real-time viewing between these devices.

Codec   An acronym for COmpressor-DECompressor. Codecs are types of video converters that are used to encode specific information into an image for transfer and then used to help decode that information for playback.

Collage   A single image created by combining multiple display devices. Using a video signal, the image will be spanned across all of the individual devices so that only a portion of the image is visible on any one device. Together, they make the whole picture.

Component   Analog video signal consisting of 3 separate signals, which may be either RGB or YUV. When component video is comprised of RGB, it also includes separate signals for *sync*, referred to as H (*horizontal*) and V (*vertical*).

Composite   Analog video signal consisting of one channel of standard definition video.

Compositing   Video editing term referring to combining multiple layers of video images into a single video image for rendering and/or playback.

Contrast   A measurement of the luminance to intensity ratio that generates the level of white signal of an image.

DirectX   A Microsoft specification that dictates how gaming and video components in apps interact with each other.

DLP   Acronym for Digital Light Processing. DLP refers to a type of micromirror technology used in projectors.

DMX 512   A standard of communication protocol used in lighting consoles. Based on a network of universes, each universe can control up to 512 individual channels. DMX is an acronym for Digital MultipleX.

DMX Address   The 3-digit number assigned to a fixture that represents the first (starting) channel of that fixture's DMX footprint. The address is used to patch the fixture into the lighting console.

DMX Universe   A single communication link used for transmitting DMX control information to each channel patched to it. It is comprised of 512 DMX channels.

Dotcrawl   A video artifact that has an appearance similar to an animated checkerboard.

DVI   An acronym for Digital Visual Interface. Single-link DVI can support resolutions up to 1920×1200; Dual-link DVI can support up to 2560×1600.

EDID   An acronym for Extended Display Identification Data. EDID allows resolution and refresh rate data to be exchanged between the display device and the computer.

Ethernet Switch   A device used to connect networking equipment (i.e. computers). Switches do not broadcast all data to all ports; instead, a switch provides each connected device with its own link and only data specific to that port is transmitted.

Fixture Personality (Profile)   The mapping of every attribute of an automated lighting fixture to a DMX control channel; every fixture has a unique DMX profile based on its DMX protocol.

Frame Interpolation   Best described as frame blending, interpolation smooths out the choppiness between two frames of a media clip when slowed down by mathematically averaging the motion between two frames and "inserting" this data as a new frame between the two existing frames.

Gamma   A mathematical relationship between the perceived brightness of a pixel in an image and the actual brightness value of the pixel; it is used to correct for the light sensitivity of the human eye and controls how the range of tonal values in an image appear to the human eye when shown on a display device.

Genlock   A reference signal used to synchronize all video devices for simultaneous playback. It is commonly used in television/broadcast applications.

GPU   An acronym for Graphics Processing Unit. The GPU was designed to handle the math-intensive tasks required by 3D modeling and CAD applications.

HDD   An acronym for Hard Disk Drive.

HDMI An acronym for High-Definition Multimedia Interface. HDMI is a digital video and audio interface commonly used in consumer electronics.

HMap2 A component created by Green Hippo that allows bidirectional communication between a Hippotizer and an HMap2 compatible lighting console.

Image Blending The process of spanning a single image across multiple projectors. When a single image is divided into sections and distributed out to individual projectors, the image will need to be reassembled by aligning the separate images and then overlapping the images slightly (and imperceptibly) so that it appears as one single image. Most projectors have an image blending setting, and many media servers also allow you to make adjustments to the area of image overlap in order to fine-tune the blend.

Image Compression The process of reducing the file size of an image without changing the overall resolution and/or dimensions of the image.

Interlacing If a media clip is compressed using interlacing, alternating lines of the image will be drawn per each consecutive frame, as in first even lines in frame 1, then odd lines in frame 2.

IP Address An acronym for Internet Protocol address, this is a unique number assigned to each computer or device connected via a network.

Keystoning Image distortion caused by projecting an image from any angle other than 90 degrees perpendicular between the lens and the surface.

LED An acronym for Light Emitting Diode; the LED is a single point source of light that emits a single color. Additional colors can be created via the combination of individual RGB LEDs. LEDs are popular for video because they are bright, they use very little power, and they give off very little heat.

Letterbox Aspect ratio format better known as "widescreen" or 16:9. If a 4:3 ratio is transferred to a 16:9 ratio, then the top and bottom of the screen will be filled with black space to preserve the image's original aspect ratio.

Lumens The measurement of the amount of light produced by a light source (lamp).

Luminance The measurement of brightness of a light source or a reflective surface.

Macro (as applies to a lighting programmer) A series of keystrokes of functions stored into a single button that executes all of the keystrokes when activated.

Media Library (as relates to a media server) A folder in a computer that contains the individual clips of media that will be used in the show.

Media Server (as applies to a lighting programmer) A computer that contains an application that enables images and videos to be triggered via lighting cues from a lighting console or stand-alone application.

MIDI An acronym for Musical Instrument Digital Interface; this is a communication protocol that allows computers and musical devices to be connected and controlled via event messages like "ON" or "OFF". MIDI can be used as an alternative to DMX for controlling a media server.

Moiré   A digital artifact that results when two sets of parallel lines are overlaid at a slight angle.

MSEX   An acronym for Media Server Extensions, this is a communication protocol that allows for the exchange of video thumbnails between a media server and a lighting console.

MTC   Acronym for MIDI Time Code. MTC is a timecode used to synchronize multiple devices via generated MIDI messages embedded into time references.

Nit   A measurement of brightness used commonly when describing the brightness of an LED wall. The unit of measurement equals one candela per square meter.

OpenGL   The industry standard interface developed by Silicon Graphics that defines how 2D and 3D computer graphics are rendered.

211

Pixel   A single point in a digital image that contains color and luminance data.

Pixelation   Digital distortion that results from increasing the scale of an image to the point where the image begins to separate into individual blocks of pixels.

Pixel Mapping   The process of creating an assignment of pixels to specific lighting fixtures and/or LEDs based on a map generated in the media server.

Progressive Scan   Also known as *non-interlaced scanning*, this method of drawing each frame of a video image involves drawing all lines of each frame. The majority of media servers prefer non-interlaced media content for playback.

RAID An acronym for Redundant Array of Independent Disks, this is a method of combining multiple hard drives into a single storage disk.

Raster The rectangular area of pixels on a display device.

RCA A type of connector commonly found in consumer electronics to carry both audio and video signals. If you have seen the red, yellow, and white cables that come with your DVD player, then you have seen the RCA connector.

Refresh Rate The number of times the image on a display device is redrawn every second. The measurement is displayed in Hertz (Hz).

Resolution The resolution of an image refers to the number of pixels in an image.

RGB An acronym for Red, Green, Blue. A color mixing system wherein the three primary colors of light are added together to create all other possible colors. This is the primary color mixing system for LED technology.

Ringing A distortion in video playback that is caused by undesirable signal reflections, resulting in duplicates of an image that are superimposed over the image but offset so that the image appears to "ghost" or echo itself.

rpm An acronym for Revolutions Per Minute. Computer hard drives, CD drives and DVD drives are rated in rpm.

SATA An acronym for Serial ATA, this is a type of computer bus interface that allows for data transfer between the computer and a peripheral.

Scaler A scaler is used to change the size or resolution of a video signal to another size or resolution.

Scan Converter   Converts the refresh rate (e.g. 50 Hz to 60 Hz) and/or format (e.g. DVI to SDI) of a video signal to another rate or format.

SCSI (aka SCUZZY)   An acronym for Small Computer System Interface, SCSI is a set of standards for data transfer between computers and peripherals. It is outdated in contemporary computer technology, having been more or less replaced by USB.

SDI   An acronym for Serial Digital Interface. SDI is used to transmit uncompressed video signal over distances up to 300 ft/92 m.

SMPTE   An acronym for Society of Motion Picture and Television Engineers, SMPTE timecode assigns each frame of a video a timecode reference value so that it can be easily edited and/or synchronized with external audio or video sources.

SSD   An acronym for Solid State Drive, an SSD is a storage hard drive that contains no spinning disc; therefore, it has a fast read time and is not as susceptible to being dropped as an HDD.

213

Subnet Mask   A 32-bit number that masks an IP address, and divides the IP address into network address and host address.

Switcher (common term for *video switcher*)   A video switcher is used to switch between video source inputs.

Syphon   Communication protocol created for applications on MAC OSX that allows media applications to share video between them.

Transcoding   A digital conversion from one format to another, as in transcoding from MPEG-2 to H.264.

TRS   An acronym for Tip, Ring, Sleeve. TRS is a type of audio connector that contains three contacts and is commonly used in audio cables.

UV Map   A 2D representation of each of the surfaces of a 3D object that specifies a certain area of a video image will appear on a specific area of the 3D object when displayed.

Vertices (Vertex)   A point that represents the intersection of a shape and can be used to manipulate the shape when working with 3D objects.

VGA   An acronym for Video Graphics Array, VGA cables carry an analog video signal and have a maximum resolution of 2048 × 1536 (QXGA).

Video Capture Card   A type of video card for a computer that allows a video signal from an external source to be input into an application and "captured" for use.

XLR   A type of connector commonly used in audio and lighting cables. Audio XLR cables typically have three pins, while DMX lighting cables typically have five pins.

YUV   A color encoding process where Y represents brightness, while U and V represent the color components of a video signal. Commonly used in television broadcast applications, each of the three parts of the signal are compressed for transmission.

The list of products below feature the latest digital media and lighting control technology available.

SOFTWARE ONLY

- ArKaos® MediaMaster™ Pro www.arkaos.net
- MADMapper™ www.madmapper.com
- MADRIX® www.madrix.com
- Mbox® Studio www.prg.com/
- Modul8™ www.garagecube.com
- PixelMAD™ www.catvx.com
- PixelDrive™ www.radlite.com/pixeldrive.html
- Quartz Composer https://developer.apple.com/technologies/mac/graphics-and-animation.html
- RasterMapper™ cled.barcousa.com/support.html
- Resolume™ 4 Arena www.resolume.com

MEDIA SERVERS WITH HARDWARE

- Ai® www.avolitesmedia.com
- ArKaos® MediaMaster™ Pro www.arkaos.net
- Axon® www.highend.com
- Catalyst® www.catvx.com
- d3® www.d3tech.com
- grandMA® VPU www.malighting.com
- Hippotizer™ www.green-hippo.com
- Maxedia™ Compact Rackmount www.martin.com
- Mbox® Designer www.prg.com
- Pandoras Box www.coolux.de

LIGHTING CONSOLE INTEGRATED/ PROPRIETARY PACKAGES

- Avo Sapphire® Media Control Surface (proprietary for Ai® control) www.avolitesmedia.com
- ChamSys® MagicQ (CITP, Pixel Mapper Engine) www.chamsysusa.com
- MA Lighting grandMA2 (HMap2, CITP, Bitmap Effects®) www.malighting.com
- Jands® Vista™ (CITP) www.jands.com
- Martin® M1 (CITP, MaxNet) www.martin.com
- PRG V676® (CITP) www.prg.com

Notes

1. Vickie Claiborne, "Video Digerati: Convergence 101," *Pro Lights and Staging News* January 2006, 36.
2. ———, "Video Digerati: Video in Captivity," *Pro Lights and Staging News* September 2006, 52.
3. ———, "Video Digerati: The Eternal Question: MAC or PC?" *Pro Lights and Staging News* October 2011, 76.
4. ———, "Video Digerati: Programming with a Media Server," *Pro Lights and Staging News* June 2006, 38.
5. ———, "Video Digerati: DVI: Digital Video to Go," *Pro Lights and Staging News* July 2008, 43.
6. ———, "Video Digerati: Programming with a Media Server," *Pro Lights and Staging News* June 2006, 38.
7. ———, "Video Digerati: Personality Counts," *Pro Lights and Staging News* May 2007, 47.
8. ———, "Video Digerati: You Say You Want a Resolution," *Pro Lights and Staging News* April 2006, 40.
9. ———, "Video Digerati: Let's Talk Content," *Pro Lights and Staging News* May 2006, 36.
10. ———, "Video Digerati: Pretty as a Pixel," *Pro Lights and Staging News* August 2006, 46.
11. ———, "Video Digerati: The Clear Reality of HD," *Pro Lights and Staging News* November 2007, 82.
12. ———, "Video Digerati: Let's Talk Content," *Pro Lights and Staging News* May 2006, 36.
13. ———, "Video Digerati: Programming with a Media Server," *Pro Lights and Staging News* June 2006, 38.
14. ———, "Video Digerati: You Say You Want a Resolution," *Pro Lights and Staging News* April 2006, 40.
15. ———, "Video Digerati: Taking the Frame Blender off Choppy," *Pro Lights and Staging News* December 2006, 41.
16. ———, "Video Digerati: Content Creation Software," *Pro Lights and Staging News* November 2008, 57.
17. ———, "Video Digerati: Preparing Your Digital Media Server for a Show," *Pro Lights and Staging News* February 2006, 36.

Notes

18. ———, "Video Digerati: CYA with CMA," *Pro Lights and Staging News* November 2006, 44.

19. ———, "Video Digerati: CITP is MSEXY," *Pro Lights and Staging News* July 2009, 31.

20. ———, "Video Digerati: 3D Mapping," *Pro Lights and Staging News* September 2010, 37.

21. ———, "Video Digerati: The Master Rapper Mapper," *Pro Lights and Staging News* September 2008, 60.

22. ———, "Video Digerati: Help, I'm Synching!" *Pro Lights and Staging News* October 2006, 66.

23. ———, "Video Digerati: 3D Mapping," *Pro Lights and Staging News* September 2010, 37.

24. ———, "Video Digerati: Pixel Mapping," *Pro Lights and Staging News* May 2009, 35.

25. ———, "Video Digerati: Rediscovering MIDI," *Pro Lights and Staging News* July 2013, 38.

26. ———, "Video Digerati: DMX-Controlled Digital Moving Lights," *Pro Lights and Staging News* January 2007, 35.

27. ———, "Video Digerati: Moving Yoke LED Fixtures," *Pro Lights and Staging News* September 2009, 37.

28. ———, "Video Digerati: Countdowns & Confetti: Prepping Media for New Year's Eve," *Pro Lights and Staging News* January 2011, 36.

Bibliography

Claiborne, Vickie, January 2006. Video Digerati: Convergence 101. Pro Lights and Staging News, 36.

———, February 2006. Video Digerati: Preparing Your Digital Media Server for a Show. Pro Lights and Staging News, 36.

———, April 2006. Video Digerati: You Say You Want a Resolution. Pro Lights and Staging News, 40.

———, May 2006. Video Digerati: Let's Talk Content. Pro Lights and Staging News, 36.

———, June 2006. Video Digerati: Programming with a Media Server. Pro Lights and Staging News, 38.

———, August 2006. Video Digerati: Pretty as a Pixel. Pro Lights and Staging News, 46.

———, September 2006. Video Digerati: Video in Captivity. Pro Lights and Staging News, 52.

———, October 2006. Video Digerati: Help, I'm Synching!. Pro Lights and Staging News, 66.

———, November 2006. Video Digerati: CYA with CMA. Pro Lights and Staging News, 44.

———, December 2006. Video Digerati: Taking the Frame Blender off Choppy. Pro Lights and Staging News, 41.

———, January 2007. Video Digerati: DMX-Controlled Digital Moving Lights. Pro Lights and Staging News, 35.

———, May 2007. Video Digerati: Personality Counts. Pro Lights and Staging News, 47.

———, November 2007. Video Digerati: The Clear Reality of HD. Pro Lights and Staging News, 82.

———, July 2008. Video Digerati: DVI: Digital Video to Go. Pro Lights and Staging News, 43.

———, September 2008. Video Digerati: The Master Rapper Mapper. Pro Lights and Staging News, 60.

———, November 2008. Video Digerati: Content Creation Software. Pro Lights and Staging News, 57.

———, May 2009. Video Digerati: Pixel Mapping. Pro Lights and Staging News, 35.

———, July 2009. Video Digerati: CITP is MSEXY. Pro Lights and Staging News, 31.

———, September 2009. Video Digerati: Moving Yoke LED Fixtures. Pro Lights and Staging News, 37.

———, September 2010. Video Digerati: 3D Mapping. Pro Lights and Staging News, 37.

———, January 2011. Video Digerati: Countdowns & Confetti: Prepping Media for New Year's Eve. Pro Lights and Staging News, 36.

———, October 2011. Video Digerati: The Eternal Question: MAC or PC? Pro Lights and Staging News, 76.

———, July 2013. Video Digerati: Rediscovering MIDI. Pro Lights and Staging News, 38.

Index

Page numbers in **bold** refer to figures

221

Index